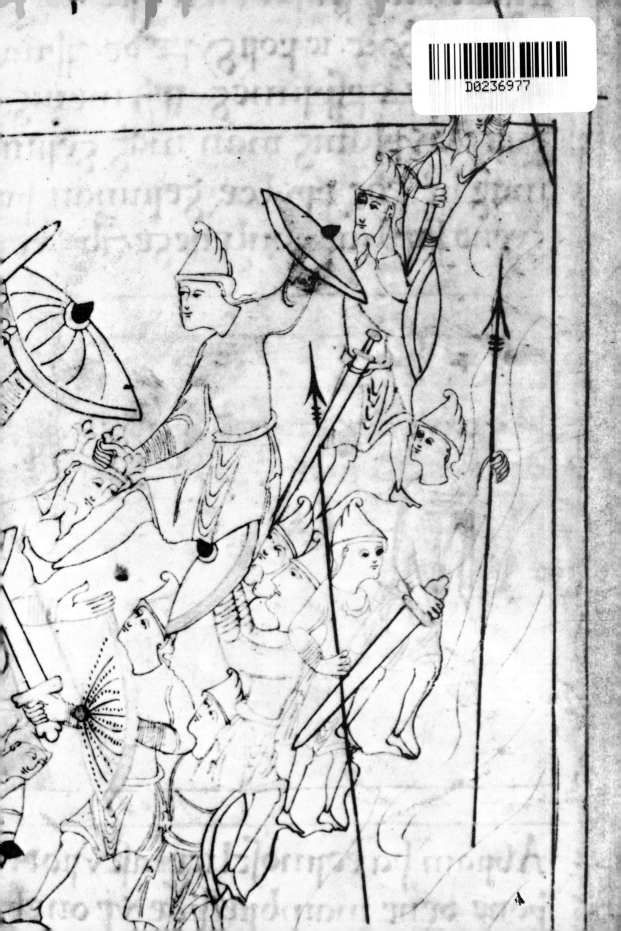

The Life and Times of
ALFRED THE GREAT

The Life and Times of

ALFRED THE GREAT

Douglas Woodruff

Introduction by Antonia Fraser

Book Club Associates, London

To Penelope Betjeman,
In memory of her Wantage years

Picture research by Anne Garrels
House editor: Celia Clear
House art editor: Tim Higgins
Series designed by Paul Watkins
Layout by Margaret Downing

Filmset by Keyspools Limited, Golborne, Lancs
Printed and bound in Great Britain by
Morrison & Gibb Ltd, London & Edinburgh

Contents

Introduction

No OTHER KING IN OUR HISTORY has been honoured with the epithet of Great. In this respect Alfred was and is unique. Douglas Woodruff, in a brilliant survey of Alfred's career and his place in English history, justifies this accolade given to the man who, in the ninth century, was in effect the founder of the English monarchy. He demonstrates that essentially Alfred's triumph was one of character: perhaps it is for this, with our natural English preoccupation with such virtues as determination, patience and courage in adversity, that we have taken Alfred so warmly into the depths of our national consciousness?

Certainly Alfred suffered enough adversity in youth; there were personal matters such as his lowly position in the family – he was the youngest of four brothers all of whom became kings – and his chronic ill-health; then there were the wider implications of the grim situation into which he was born, with his native Wessex harried by those Northmen who for nearly a century had been plaguing the remnants of the Roman Empire. Even the famous story of the burnt cakes is not necessarily improbable in that it illustrates the wretched plight into which the Wessex dynasty had fallen. A studious disposition, later much tenacity and skill in military matters, and forethought which has lead him to be termed 'the father of the British Navy', a strong command of the wise principles of government including law-giving and the encouragement of learning: these were the qualities which brought Alfred to success. And there was another quality on which Douglas Woodruff casts much interesting light, Alfred's keen religious sense, springing from the central place which he accorded to Christ in his world, an inspiration which may have dated from his original visit to Rome as a young child.

In spite of the distance of time which separates us from Alfred – over a thousand years – he emerges from Douglas Woodruff's felicitous narrative not only with the conventional attributes of a strong ruler but also with an engaging personality of his own. 'Now no man can administer government unless he have fit tools and the raw materials to work upon . . . and a king's raw materials and the instruments of rule are a well-peopled land, and he must have men of prayer, men of war, and men of work': Alfred's philosophy is seen in glosses such as this on the various famous works which he caused to be translated and disseminated in Anglo-Saxon. It was typical of Alfred that he looked forward to his own death, which occurred when he was in his fifties (worn out no doubt by the hard nature of his existence) with intellectual curiosity, wanting to enjoy 'that endless life where all shall be made clear'. The attitude was characteristic of the man who had declared his intention 'to live worthily as long as I live, and after my life to leave to them that should come after, my memory in good works'.

Antonia Fraser

Acknowledgments

Photographs and illustrations are supplied by, or reproduced by kind permission of the following: Aerofilms: 68–9; Anderson: 28–9; Antivarisk Topografiska Arkivet, Stockholm: 57, 58, 90/1, 91/1, 128; Ashmolean Museum: *96*, 122, *174–5*, 178, 202/1, 202/2, 203/1, 203/2; Bibliothèque Nationale: 106; Bildarchive Foto Marburg: 23/3, 168; Bodleian Library: 72, 102, 145, 159, 187, 194, 195; British Museum: 10–11, 23/1, 34, 35, 42, 43, 44, 45, 52–3, 54–5, 61, 65/2, 70–71, 76, 79, 82–3, *84*, *93*, 94, 98/2, 100/1, 100/2, 105, 108–9, 110, 121, 123/2, 126/2, 130, *130–131*, *132*, 133, 148, 149, 162, 172, *177*, *180*, 184, 185, *189*, *192*, 196; Bundesdenkmalamt, Vienna: 127; Caisse Nationale des Monuments Historiques, Paris: 155; Master and Fellows of Corpus Christi College, Cambridge: 18; Department of the Environment (Crown Copyright): 208–9; C.M.Dixon: 62, 126/1; Durham Cathedral Library: *142/2*, *143*; Françoise Foliot: 40, 65; Green Studio, Dublin: 138; Guildhall Museum: 91/2; André Held: 32; Illustrated London News: 49; A.F.Kersting: 165, 170, 206, 211; London Museum: 64/1, 64/2, 64/3, 65/1, 65/3; Mansell Collection: 157; Museum of Ireland: 50; National Monuments Record: 87, 136–7, 166/1, 166/2, 167/1, 167/2, 171/1, 171/2, 171/3; Osterreichische Nationalbibliothek: 23/2; Phoebus Picture Library: *81*, 99/2; Scala: 31; Service de documentation photographiques, Paris: 22; Stadtbildstelle, Aachen: 13; Stift Kremsmünster: 51; Trinity College Library, Dublin: *14*; Universitetets Oldsaksamling Oslo: 75, 90/1, 90/2, 98/2, 99/1; University Museum of Archaeology, Cambridge: 141; Utrecht University Library: 24–5; Victoria and Albert Museum: 142/1, 198–9, 201; Winchester City Museum: 182.

Numbers in italics refer to colour illustrations.

Maps designed by Tim Higgins and drawn by Design Practitioners Limited.

9

1 The Wessex Dynasty

AMONG THE MANY THOUSANDS of kings and emperors and other rulers of men in our Western civilisation, posterity and the common consent of mankind has been most sparing in conferring the splendid epithet 'the Great'. In 3,000 years, taking us back towards the dawn of recorded history, it would be hard to name twenty to whom the title is universally granted. After Cyrus the Great and Alexander the Great in antiquity and Pompey and Herod at the dawn of the Christian era, the Roman Empire produces only Constantine, and the Western Empire the Frankish Charlemagne or Charles the Great, and the German Otto I. Only three Popes qualify of all the long line of 260, St Leo I, St Gregory I and St Nicholas I. In modern times, the eighteenth century produces Frederick II of Prussia, the Tsar Peter and the Tsarina Catherine, but the title has somehow never stuck to Henry of Navarre or his grandson Louis XIV, or to Napoleon despite the efforts of patriotic French historians. There is one monk from Asia Minor, the founder of Eastern monasticism, St Basil; one medieval philosopher, the Rhinelander Albertus Magnus. There are men who are called the Great Captain, or the Great Condé, but that is not quite the same. The list shows that posterity can be capricious with Pompey in it, but neither Julius Caesar nor Augustus, though they are historically incomparably more important. On the whole, it is remarkable how seldom the courtiers and the contemporaries who have flattered men of great power have managed to give them this lasting title.

But in this small company this island produces one name, that of Alfred, King of the West Saxons from 871 to 901: Alfred the Great. The title was slow in coming – it is post-medieval – but it has stuck. By contrast with the enormous stage on which Constantine or Charlemagne performed and carried through their enduring immense decisions, King Alfred is almost reminiscent of Robinson Crusoe, in that the romance of his story comes out of the poverty of his resources; none of the other rulers who have earned the title 'the Great' have had to contend with such exiguous lack of means of every kind, have ruled so small a territory or have faced such adversity. But his is, all the same, a success story, a triumph of character, which is why his countrymen, who were quick to recognise his pre-eminence in his lifetime, have never forgotten him. His ultimate achievement

The artistic development
of Saxon England cannot
be clearly distinguished
from that of Celtic
Ireland because the early
illuminated manuscripts
are written in Irish
'half-uncials' and contain a
blend of Celtic and
Anglo-Saxon features.
Furthermore the source of
a manuscript is often
uncertain since books
sometimes came to rest
far from their place of origin

The two manuscripts
illustrated here, the *Book of
Durrow* (left) and the
Book of Kells (right) both
ended up in Ireland but
may have been illuminated
in England. In each case
the figure depicted is
St Matthew. The interlace
border of the
seventh-century *Book of
Durrow* reflects pagan
tradition, for in the
previous century interlace
had been characteristic of
the illustrations of the
armour of pagan heroes.
The *Book of Kells* dates
from the ninth century
and is the most elaborate
and brilliant of the early
Gospel Books. It may have
been taken to Kells
from Iona when the
Viking raids began.

was the foundation of the English monarchy. Having saved Wessex, which was then all England south of the Thames, Alfred left his son Edward in a position to bring the Midlands, Mercia, under his control, and his grandson, Athelstan, to establish his authority, although not without constant challenge, as far as the Scottish border, making him the first English king to invade Scotland. Athelstan's nephew, Edgar, consolidated this authority, so that even when the disastrous reign of Edgar's son, Ethelred the Unready, had led to the anomaly of three Danish kings ruling England, Canute ruled from the south northwards, from Alfred's city of Winchester. There can be no clearer proof that it was the Wessex monarchy which had become the English monarchy. When Canute's sons died young, there was general agreement to call to the throne Ethelred's son, Edward the Confessor, with whom the direct line of Alfred ends.

That in essence was Alfred's great political achievement. But many kings have established dynasties which have endured, often without themselves having inherited a crown, and if that had been all that Alfred had done, he would hardly have been accorded the title of 'Great'. That is a more personal tribute to his elevation of character, the largeness of his views, the range of his constructive energy. It is because we know so much about him, because all succeeding generations had known more about him than about the rest of his family, that he has struck the imagination of posterity. This was never more marked than in Queen Victoria's reign when all things Germanic were in high favour. When the thousand years were completed in 1871, there was a great burst of literary enthusiasm for King Alfred. Statues were erected at Wantage, Winchester, London and, on a smaller scale, at Pewsey in Wiltshire. There was even more enthusiasm in 1901 for the millenary of his death, and a great deal of generous and inspiring rhetoric was poured out, as will be discussed in the final chapter of this book. It made the English feel particularly proud that they could look back on a thousand years of a national history which culminated in the immense British Empire with which the twentieth century opened.

But already the occasion of 1901 was used by careful scholars to look more closely into the sources on which our knowledge

16

of Alfred is based. This process has continued, and after three-quarters of a century of minute Anglo-Saxon scholarship, it has become for the moment disconcertingly possible that our ancestors took Alfred at his own valuation. The sources on which we and later chroniclers and the like had to rely, the *Anglo-Saxon Chronicle*, and his chaplain Asser's life of his patron, have been shown by minute investigation to have been written under the King's close supervision from materials he himself supplied, or with the intention of pleasing him. Alfred was, in fact, a master of what we tend to think of as the twentieth century's invented calling, public relations. Generations of historians have taken his words at their face value without allowing for the human factor, the natural desire of all public men to present themselves in the most favourable light, perhaps to be jealous in giving credit to others, to want the limelight for themselves, not to minimise the dangers and difficulties they have overcome, or what they have achieved. We have to look at the sources for Alfred's life and works with our critical faculties on the alert, but at the same time we can evaluate what he did by the light of subsequent history, and we can also draw a profitable comparison by the study of his contemporaries on the mainland of Europe. At the end we shall conclude that if he boasted and subtly presented the facts as he wished them to be remembered, that does not undermine the reality of his great achievement and the justice of the special place he has been accorded in our history, or diminish the originality and goodness of his character and the range of his ideas.

We have, in addition to the *Anglo-Saxon Chronicle* which he supervised, a biography written by Asser, his chaplain. Asser came from South Wales, was a monk and possibly something higher in rank, even Bishop of St David's in Pembrokeshire. That he came from Wales is an indication how few and far between were learned men in Alfred's time, and how far afield he had to seek for them. He rewarded Asser with a see in Wessex, Sherborne, then a see of great importance, and he also gave him charge of the monastery at Amesbury. Asser for his part has been one of the chief architects of Alfred's fame, for he has enabled us to know him as we know no other member of his House. As his life continued to be known and read, and

micel ſciphere · ⁊ . . . . ⁊þiſſene here ɜeſluhton

an dccc·lxii oſpic aldoꝝ man mid þam uin ſcire ⁊ eþelpulf aldoꝝmon mid bearu

an dccc·lxiii puc ſcire · þone here ɜeꝼliandon ⁊ þæl ſcope ɜeſild ahton · ⁊ re eþel

an dccc·lxiiii burht pucrode · u · ɜdp · ⁊ hiſ liclip · æt ſcire bupindeꝛ ᛭

an dccc·lxv Her ꝼæt heþen here on tenet · ⁊ ɜ namon · ⁊ piþ pip cant pdpum ɜdanſpa
no · lū ꝼeoh ɜeheton · piþ þa ꝼruþe · ⁊ under þā ꝼruþe · ⁊ þā ꝼeoh ɜ hate
rehſce hiſne · on niht up beſtel · ⁊ oꝝ hitſ ɜedde alle . . ceht eaſtſpeaꝛde

an dccc·lxvi Her ꝼenɜ eþeꝛed eþelbꝛi hiſ bꝛoþur to ɜeꝼeabend ꝛice · ⁊ þi ilcan ɜea
re · cū micel here on anɜel cꝛnnɜ lond ⁊ pintꝛ ſetl namon on eaſt
englū ⁊ þæꝛ ɜe horſude · pundon · ⁊ hie him ꝼriþ namon ᛬

an dccc·lxvii Her ꝼoꝛon ꝼe here oꝼ eaſt englū oꝼeꝛ humbꝛe muþan to eoꝼor pic ceaſ
tre · on noꝛþ hymbꝛe · ⁊ þæꝛ þæꝛ micel un ꝼaþineſ þæꝛe þeode betꝑxū
him ſelꝼū ⁊ hie hæ dun hiꝛa cꝛninɜ · up oꝛpen ne oſbꝛiht · ⁊ unɜe
cindne cꝛninɜ · undꝛ hyꝛzon ellan · ⁊ hie ſitre · onɜeaþ re copil ɜecꝛipdon
þæt hie piþ þone here ꝼinnide þe þæꝛ uir · ⁊ hie þeth micle ꝼiꝛhd ɜ̄ɜadno
don · ⁊ þone here ꝼohton · æt boꝛon pio ceaſtꝛo · ⁊ on pieaſtꝛe bꝛecon
⁊ hie ſume inne pundon · ⁊ þæꝛ pæꝛ unɜimet lic peþ ɜ ſlæɜen noꝛþan
beꝛɜ . . hꝛmbꝛa ſume binnan ſume burdan ⁊ þa lꝛiniɜ ꝼe beɜ̄ oꝼſlæɜene
⁊ þio laꝼe piþ þone here ꝼꝛiþ nāmin · ⁊ þi ilcan ɜeaꝛe ɜeꝼoꝛ edelhſtan biſc̄
ꝼeh . . ꝼde þæt . . byꝛe ꝼice · ⁊ þin ꝼæt æt ſcire bupinan ⁊ hiſ liclip þæꝛon
tune ᛬

an dccc·lxviii Her ꝼoꝛ ꝼe ilcd here ſinnan miþce · to ſno tenɜaliſd · ⁊ þæꝛ pintꝛ ſetl
namon · ⁊ buꝛɜꝛed miþcend cꝛninɜ · ⁊ hiſ pioten bedon eþeꝛed þæſ
ſecend cꝛninɜ · ⁊ elꝼꝛed hiſ bꝛoþuꝛ þæt hie him ɜeſultum addon
þæt hie piþ þone here ɜeꝼuhtᵒn · ⁊ þa ꝼendon hie · mid pe ꝛeþend ꝼiɜ h
de ſinnan miþce · oꝼ ſno tenɜ hid · ⁊ þone here pæꝛ metton on þam̄
ɜeboꝛc · ⁊ þæꝛ nan hæþlic ɜeꝼolc ne ɜedlp · ⁊ miþce ꝼꝛiþ nāmon piþ þone

an dccc·lxix Her ꝼoꝛ ꝼohɜio · eꝼt to boꝛon pic ceaſtꝛe · ⁊ þæꝛ ꝼæt · i · ɜdp ᛬ ⁊ hie ꝼe

an dccc·lxx Her ꝛad ꝼe hɜio oꝼꝛ miþce ſinnan eaſt enɜle · ⁊ pintꝛ ꝼæl nd namon ·
æt þeod ꝼoꝛd d · þiꝛ pint eadmund cꝛninɜ hiſ piþ ꝼeatte · ⁊ þa d eniſcan
ſiɜe nāmon · ⁊ þone cꝛninɜ oꝼ ſlaɜon · ⁊ þæt lond all ɜeeodon · ⁊ þiꝛ ed
þe ɜeoꝛ edulioþ atce biſce · ⁊ ɜeheneþ picaun ſciꝛe biſceoppꝛcaþ ɜeopenī

an dccc·lxxi Her cuom ſehere to ældinɜum · on peſt ſeaxe · ⁊ þæſ ꝛmb · iii · niht pidon
ii · coꝛldaꝝ up pazen ate · hie eþelpuhe aldoꝛman en on enɜla ꝼeld d · ⁊ hi
pæþ piþ ɜ̄ɜeadite · ⁊ ɜ̄ɜnid aim þæꝛ · r · b · iiii · niht · eþeꝛed cꝛninɜ ⁊ elꝼꝛed
hiꝛ bꝛoþuꝛ þæꝛ micle ꝼiꝛhd to ꝛældinɜū ɜeleddon ⁊ þiþ þone heꝛeɜ

because Alfred was known to be zealous for learning, all sorts of Anglo-Saxon proverbs were attributed to him and circulated in the Middle Ages as those of Alfred. In a great medieval poem of the fourteenth century, Laymon's *Brut*, Alfred is called England's darling. He was, in short, the best remembered and known, as well as the most highly esteemed of the pre-Conquest kings. In the England that was being ruled by Continental dynasties, the Normans and Plantagenets, and as English national feeling grew in vigour and self-confidence and absorbed the French-speaking military caste, pride in England carried Alfred along with it, so that his fame never really diminished. If there was ever a period of eclipse it came very early, when men were lauding his great-grandson, Edgar the Peaceable.

Military success was an essential part of Alfred's story, but in the perspective of history he is to be looked at as not only saving the kingdom he inherited from being over-run and partitioned among the Danes. He married a Mercian, and he prepared for the absorption of Mercia by his son and of the whole of England by his grandson, so that within forty years of his death, the English monarchy was held in high regard on the mainland of Europe, and three of Alfred's grand-daughters became the wives of European rulers: the first of Otto the Great, who was to revive the empire of Charlemagne; another of Charles the Simple of the failing Carolingian line; and a third of Hugh Capet, founder of the great House of Capet which was to rule France down to the French Revolution. These marriages place Alfred in the genealogy of all the royal houses of Europe, as they inter-married.

Yet the story begins very quietly and inauspiciously in the royal *vill* at the foot of the Berkshire Downs, where the town of Wantage now stands. Anglo-Saxon building was of wood, seldom of stone, and all traces of the royal residence have disappeared, but we can be sure it was near the parish church which was always the fixed point in old settlements, either on the high ground which is now the market-place, with his statue, or perhaps, more probably, to the north of the parish church where there is a stream of water which runs through land which was for many years the home of the Poet Laureate John Betjeman.

OPPOSITE A page from the *Anglo-Saxon Chronicle* describing the battle of Ashdown. Seven versions of the *Chronicle* exist, written by succeeding generations at different places. The version illustrated here was begun in Alfred's reign, continued at Winchester till 1154 and subsequently written in Canterbury.

We know that it was an important residence because it continued in use for at least 250 years. Alfred was born there around 849 and early in the eleventh century Ethelred II issued directions chiefly for Mercia which are known as the Wantage Code.

Alfred was the youngest of four brothers, the children of a remarkable father, Ethelwulf, and the grandchildren of Egbert, first of the great Wessex monarchs. Before him the West Saxons had had a confused and divided history, and at the beginning of the century in which Alfred was born, they had been subordinate to King Offa of Mercia who made vague claims to be king of all the English. That Angles, Saxons and Jutes all came from the north-west corner of Europe, where they were in some sort of touch with the outposts of the Roman Empire, is shown by the common consciousness they all had that although they might fight among themselves, these contests were of the nature of civil wars or dynastic struggles, different in kind from the conflicts with the Romanised Britons or the western Celtic peoples of Wales and Strathclyde and the Picts and Scots in the North. Bede, writing in about 730 from Northumbria, called his history the *Ecclesiastical History of the English Nation*, as though they saw themselves as one people. There was even a recognised if mainly honorary title of 'Bretwalda' or 'Paramount Ruler', which it would be too grand to call 'King of Kings'. This vague paramountcy was largely personal, but in broad terms it can be said that the Angles settled between the Humber and the Firth of Forth were the strongest kingdom in the seventh century, that the Mercians emerged in the course of the eighth century, while the ninth century was the century of Wessex, whose royal House blossomed out to be kings of all England in the tenth.

The founder of this Wessex supremacy was Alfred's grandfather, Egbert. He was of the royal blood, but monarchy among these Germanic tribes was not a matter of strict heredity; the *Witanagemot* or Council of wise men could choose, and need not necessarily take the eldest son, though it generally did so, and the instances in which the younger son succeeded were generally bloody and involving murder. At the beginning of the ninth century, Beothric held the throne of Wessex because he was married to a daughter of the great Mercian King Offa.

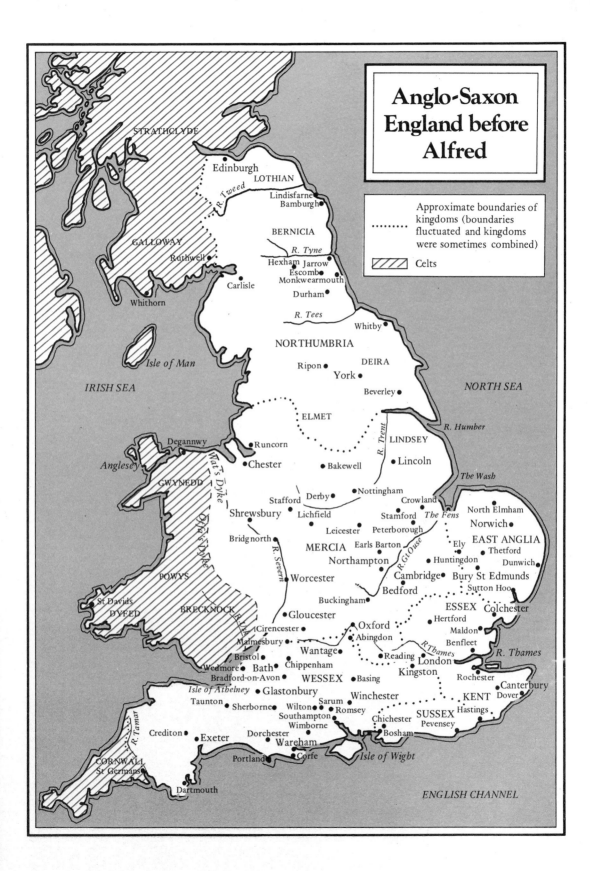

Anglo-Saxon England before Alfred

Approximate boundaries of kingdoms (boundaries fluctuated and kingdoms were sometimes combined)

Celts

STRATHCLYDE

LOTHIAN

Edinburgh

R. Tweed

Lindisfarne
Bamburgh

BERNICIA

GALLOWAY

Ruthwell

R. Tyne

Hexham Jarrow
Escomb
Monkwearmouth

Whithorn

Carlisle

Durham

R. Tees

Whitby

Isle of Man

IRISH SEA

NORTHUMBRIA

DEIRA

Ripon York

Beverley

ELMET

R. Humber

Degannwy

Runcorn

LINDSEY

Anglesey

Chester

Bakewell

Lincoln

GWYNEDD

Wat's Dyke

The Wash

Stafford Derby Nottingham

Crowland

Shrewsbury Lichfield

Stamford The Fens

North Elmham

Norwich

POWYS

Offa's Dyke

Bridgnorth

R. Severn

Leicester Peterborough

MERCIA Earls Barton

Ely EAST ANGLIA

Thetford

Dunwich

Northampton

R. Gt Ouse

Huntingdon

St Davids
DYFED

BRECKNOCK

Worcester

Cambridge Bury St Edmunds

Bedford

Sutton Hoo

Buckingham

ESSEX Colchester

Gloucester

Hertford

Cirencester

Oxford
Abingdon

Maldon

Malmesbury

Wantage

R. Thames

Benfleet

Bristol

Reading

London

R. Thames

Wedmore Bath
Bradford-on-Avon

Chippenham

Kingston

Rochester

WESSEX Basing

Canterbury

Isle of Athelney Glastonbury

Winchester

KENT Dover

Taunton Sherborne

Sarum

Romsey

Wilton

Chichester

Hastings

SUSSEX

Southampton

Pevensey

Wimborne

Bosham

Crediton

Dorchester

Exeter

Wareham

CORNWALL
St Germans

R. Tamar

Portland Corfe Isle of Wight

Dartmouth

ENGLISH CHANNEL

NORTH SEA

The Carolingian Empire

The majesty and stability of the Roman Empire was briefly revived when the Frankish king Charlemagne made his court at Aix-la-Chapelle (Aachen), and it was here Alfred's grandfather, Egbert, lived during his exile. On the death of Charlemagne's son, Louis the Pious, the empire was divided between his sons and grandsons, giving rise to France, Burgundy, Germany and Italy.

BELOW A late-ninth-century bronze statuette of Charlemagne, portraying the ideal of the monarch as soldier and judge.
RIGHT Louis the Pious depicted as defender of the faith in a book of poems from the second quarter of the ninth century.
FAR RIGHT Lothar, eldest son of Louis, inherited the imperial title but shared the imperial

lands with his brothers, Louis the German and Charles the Bald.
OPPOSITE BELOW The Octagon in the Royal Chapel, Aix-la-Chapelle, built between 792 and 805. Marble columns support richly decorated capitals in the classical style, and the vaulting is divided into triangles as in Roman architecture.

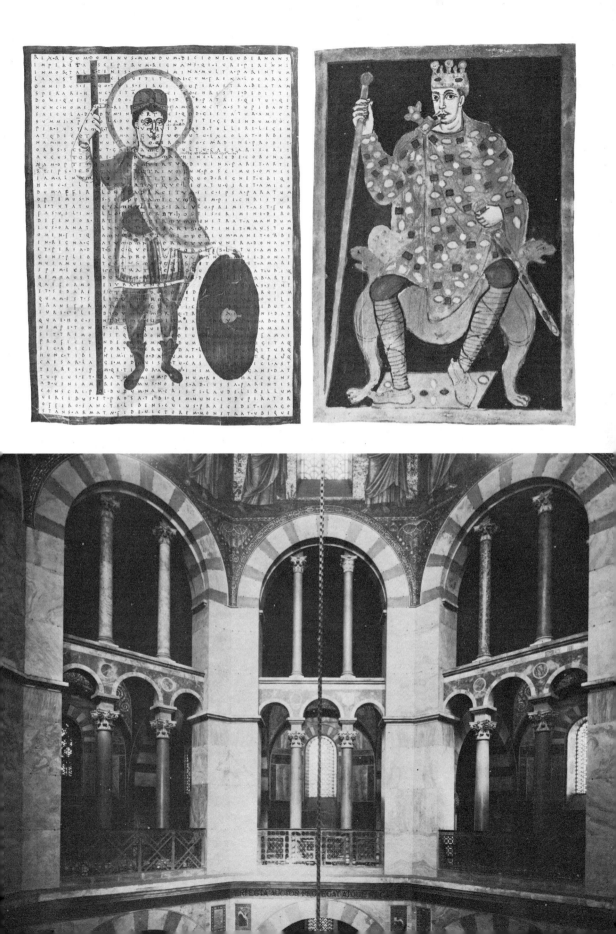

Charlemagne made his court the centre for a renaissance of art and learning, gathering craftsmen and scholars from all over Europe. The result was a flowering of culture which lasted until around 880.

The Utrecht Psalter, illustrated here, is an outstanding example of Carolingian illumination, developed from the fusion of Anglo-Saxon, Irish and Frankish techniques under the dominant influence of Byzantine painting. The psalter is from the school of Rheims *c.* 800 and is remarkable for its depth of perspective.

Egbert was driven into exile and lived for a time at the Court of Charlemagne at Aix, around the year 800 when Charlemagne had just been crowned Emperor of the West by Pope Leo III. Alfred told Asser the story of Beothric's wife. She was a dominating woman who poisoned her husband's mind against anyone she disliked, and when on occasion that did not succeed, she had recourse to real poison. It was in the course of removing in this way a young favourite of her husband that she made a mistake, and the husband as well as the favourite took the poison. She was driven from the kingdom, and Egbert was invited to the throne. Seizing all the treasure she could, Beothric's widow went to the Court of Charlemagne to seek another husband. Charlemagne does not come well out of the story which relates that he asked her whether she would be prepared to marry him or his son, and she tactlessly chose the son on the grounds that he was younger. Charlemagne, very nettled, said if she had chosen him, she could have had his son, but as it was, she would have neither. But as she had been queen, he made provision for her. He put her in charge of a convent of nuns, where she behaved so badly she was driven out, and at the last we hear of her she was destitute, with one wretched servant, and begging in the city of Padua. Because of her ill conduct, the kingdom of Wessex decreed that no woman should ever be queen, or even queen-consort, ruling with her husband, and this was thought by Alfred's biographer, Asser, to be a very exceptional and discreditable feature of the Wessex constitution. Egbert reigned for the best part of forty years.

The most important cify of Wessex was Winchester, a day's march inland from the south coast. It had a monastery as well as a bishop, and there Egbert found men whom he could promote to the two great Wessex sees of Winchester and Sherborne. Before Egbert, Kent, with the see of Canterbury, was under Mercia, as was London, but in the course of his reign Egbert acquired the same sort of influence over Mercia that Offa had wielded over Wessex in Egbert's youth. Of the notable bishops of this time the most famous was St Swithin, Bishop of Winchester until his death in 862, and to him Egbert entrusted the education of his son and heir, Ethelwulf.

There was a tenacious tradition in Winchester, recorded in

the *Book of Hyde*, that Ethelwulf himself had been both a monk and a sub-deacon. After Egbert had acquired authority over Kent, he had made Ethelwulf king there under him, but Ethelwulf, after a number of years, had retired to live the religious life in Winchester, and he had to be fetched from the cloister when Egbert died in 839 because there was no other brother to take on the responsibilities. In the form in which we have it, the *Book of Hyde* is a late compilation, but the abbey of Hyde was founded by Alfred and his son and its book is obviously full of earlier traditions and materials. It may date from the fourteenth century since the monk compiling it talks about the Dominicans being in Winchester, to which they had come only in the thirteenth century; but that is not a decisive argument against these traditions of the ninth century being true.

What is certain is that Ethelwulf was deeply religious and felt a particular devotion to the Holy See; that his first wife, who was a Jute from the Isle of Wight, was equally religious; and that Alfred, their youngest son, grew up in this atmosphere. It is extraordinary that Ethelwulf should have sent his cherished youngest child to Rome when he was no more than four years old, when it was so very common for Anglo-Saxons to die on pilgrimage in an unaccustomed climate. But we have the letter in which Pope Leo IV tells Ethelwulf that he has received his little son and invested him with the insignia and vestments of the consulship. This was an experience none of his brothers nor any other English king had in early life, and it is perhaps not fanciful to think that the impression Rome made on him accounted for the quite exceptional devotion to learning as well as to religion that was to mark him in his maturity. Pope Leo wrote about Alfred as follows:

To Ethelwulf, King of the English.

We have now graciously received your son Alfred, whom you were anxious to send at this time to the thresholds of the Holy Apostles, and we have decorated him, as a spiritual son, with the dignity of the belt and the vestments of the consulate, as is customary with Roman consuls, because he gave himself into our hands.

There can have been little prospect at that time that Alfred would one day be king, for he had at least three elder brothers,

Pope Leo IV stands on the
far left in this
ninth-century fresco of the
Ascension, from
S. Clemente Lower
Church, Rome.

28

and perhaps four, for there is a record of a son of Ethelwulf called Athelstan ruling in Kent under his father. No one could have foreseen that they would all die before they had time to leave sons old enough to be chosen by the Witan to succeed their fathers in such dangerous times. Nor had the Pope been asked to crown any king from Northumbria or Mercia or Wessex, or claimed any such right. It is probable that what was in Ethelwulf's mind was much more a spiritual relationship, that the Pope's special blessing should be given to his youngest son and that the consular dignity was a surprise, a Roman courtesy to the scion of a kingly house. But it may have been useful to Alfred in his later years that it should be believed that the holy Pope had marked him out for king. (When Alfred came to die, his eldest son, Edward, had proved himself, and there was no question who should succeed. But pretensions were put forward by a shadowy first cousin, the son of one of Alfred's brothers, who thought he had a better claim, as he had, on strict primogeniture. But while primogeniture was generally the rule, it could be varied, and in this instance Edward's own claims were reinforced by the dominating position his father had held as the saviour of his country and of a dynasty destined to go from strength to strength.)

A few years later, Alfred made a second journey to Rome, this time in the company of his father. This visit was on a much larger scale than the first. It was something Ethelwulf had been promising himself ever since he had been called to the throne in 839, and he had communicated his hopes to Charlemagne's son, the Emperor Louis the Pious, before that Emperor died in 840. He made arrangements for his two elder sons to take over the government of Wessex, Ethelbald in the west, Ethelbert in Kent, and he set out bearing rich gifts. It is a tribute to the Carolingian Empire as Charlemagne left it to his son and grandsons that in the middle of the ninth century the pilgrimage to Rome was relatively safe, that pilgrims were throughout their journey under Carolingian protection of one sort or another.

In all, Ethelwulf was away from Wessex for some two years, and these two years took for Alfred the place of the formal education which he was unable to receive at home. It is rather surprising that a bright boy, such as he undoubtedly was,

A warrior nobleman of
the ninth century, one
of a class whose power
Charlemagne increased,
depicted on a fresco in
the Oratory of
St Benedict, Rome.

should have lived so long in Rome and at the end of it be still unable to read Latin, but we must believe that this is what Asser means when he tells us that Alfred was illiterate when he was ten, for this second visit to Rome ended when he was nine.

Although he could not read Latin, he could see and listen, and Rome must have made an immense impression on him. At the time of his arrival, Pope Leo IV was fortifying what has since been known as the Leonine City, the area around St Peter's. The Vatican basilica, lying across the River Tiber, lacked the protection which the great wall of Aurelian gave to the Rome of the seven hills, and had been sacked by Saracen pirates only a few years previously. If Alfred interested himself in the measures taken to defend its church and its treasures, he would have learned that Leo IV had seen clearly that the best defence against the Saracens was to meet them at sea. Leo made alliances with cities in the south, Gaeta, Amalfi and Naples, which were similarly exposed to sea-raids and similarly prepared to build and man ships. The old Roman port of Ostia had silted up, but after one or two false starts, the history of Civita Vecchia, as the port of Rome and the home of the Pope's navy, begins at this time. Saracens who were captured were kept to work on the fortifications, as was already part of the Mohammedan tradition of sea-warfare (but it was not one which was emulated in the north, where stranded crews were slain). Leo had not only fortified the Leonine city, he had made it worth plundering again. Through Jewish merchants, he was able to buy back from the Saracens some of the jewellery and the precious stones which they had stolen, and it shows his confidence in his new fortification as well as in his reasonably strong financial position that he could do this. But his successor, Benedict III, turned to Ethelwulf, that generous-hearted king, who seemed to have plenty of money, for he had arrived in Rome with a large and splendid retinue. Ethelwulf undertook the restoration and endowment of the Saxon Hostel (now the Borgo di Sassia, on the left as you approach St Peter's), which had been burned down, probably during the Saracen raid. That such a hostel should have existed and should have been sufficiently frequented, as it plainly was, to the point of giving its name to a district, shows how much intercourse there was between Rome and England

One of the Roman churches which may have impressed Alfred is S. Prassede, built some thirty years before his visit by St Paschal I (817–24). A section of the mosaic in the apse (opposite) shows St Peter presenting St Prudenzia to Christ, with St Zeno on the right. St Prudenzia is wearing Byzantine court dress.

33

Two views of a gold and niello ring, decorated with two birds and a plant motif, bearing the name of Alfred's father, Ethelwulf. The use of niello – a black composition inlaid to give emphasis to the design – was an important technique in Anglo-Saxon jewellery. The ring was found at Laverstock in Wiltshire.

and how many pilgrims undertook the journey to the tomb of the Apostles. Although Rome was much more impressive than anything either Ethelwulf or Alfred had seen at home, they readily agreed that it was their duty as Christians to provide money for the Head of the Church, and Ethelwulf, in his will, made generous provision from his private and personal lands, as well as arranging for the tax, which was to spread from England to the mainland, known as Peter's Pence.

There are earlier payments, from Ine of Wessex, two hundred years before Ethelwulf, and Offa of Mercia a hundred years before, but what is certain is that under Ethelwulf and Alfred the payment became regular and embodied in the law. It consisted of a thirtieth part of a free man's income; it was collected by the Crown with heavy financial penalties for evasion; and it was remitted to Rome. It is also clear that the Crown collected more than it remitted. But Peter's Pence, still levied on a voluntary basis from Catholics, was stopped by Henry VIII after nearly seven hundred years. In the nineteenth century a pot of Saxon silver pennies, 830 in all, was found buried on the Palatine Hill, together with a fibula of Pope Martin II, who reigned from 942 to 946. These coins begin with Alfred but belong for the most part to the reign of his son and grandson. Why they should have been buried no one will ever know, but they prove how the custom of sending silver to Rome had taken root.

Benedict III died after three years and his successor, Nicholas I, was elected a few months after Ethelwulf and Alfred had returned home. The life of Alfred the Great spans fourteen pontificates, and in the tenth century, the darkest period in papal history, there were to be twenty-four Popes. But to the Anglo-Saxons the vicars of St Peter (not to style themselves more grandly Vicars of Christ for another two hundred years) were seen in exactly that capacity. St Peter went on in the great office regardless of who held it, and the piety towards Rome not only as holding the tombs of the great Apostles who had founded the Church there, but as the seat of authority, did not waver among Alfred's descendants. Yet the reign of Benedict III, for all its brevity, had one incident which was ominous for the future. The Carolingian who in the division of the Empire ruled in Italy, Louis II, instead of ratifying the election as the Emperor was expected to do, produced his own candidate.

The central decoration of this gold and niello ring is the *Agnus Dei* (Lamb of God), confirmed, despite the odd shape, by the letters A and D either side of the animal with abbreviation marks above them. Inside is the inscription 'Eathelswith Regina', Alfred's sister, the Queen of Mercia. This ring was found near Sherburn in Yorkshire.

35

This was a Roman ecclesiastic, Anastasius by name, who had fallen into disgrace under Leo IV, and been stripped of his offices. His reputation was so bad and the independence of the Roman electors so vital and so cherished that public opinion in Rome reacted vigorously. Louis had to abandon his attempt to intrude his nominee and had to recognise Benedict III. If, in the next century, the great local families were often to succeed in imposing their nominees on the Roman clergy, it was part of their strength that they were local and did not represent the Empire, whether it was the ruler in Byzantium or one of the rulers in the divided Western Empire. Important as Alfred's son and grandsons were to become in the dynastic life of Europe, they never succumbed to the temptations to which the Franks and the Germans were both to yield repeatedly, of trying to dominate the frequent papal elections. Until the reforms of the eleventh century, the Popes were elected by the clergy and people of Rome, and in the course of the tenth century 'the people' was a synonym for the dukes of Spoleto and the House of Tusculum, and over and over again they intruded scions of their families, often mere youths, into the Chair of Peter. In the middle of the tenth century, the abuse was so bad that Otto the Great intervened decisively. But although three of the English kings in succession were his brothers-in-law, they stood apart on these dramatic events. There was a tradition which we may surely date in its beginnings to Ethelwulf and Alfred, of a deep reverence for the Papacy, for the abiding office if not for the often unworthy holder. For their part, the Popes left the initiative for the appointment of English bishops to the King, as Charlemagne had taught them to leave such appointments to him.

Of the central place his religion played in Alfred's life, Asser gives abundant details, and they are corroborated in all that we have that emanates from Alfred himself. This will appear later in this narrative when we look at what this king did for the revival of learning at a time when learning and religion were inseparably intertwined, but we cannot understand Alfred in his other capacities, whether as a warrior, a law-giver or an administrator, unless we start by understanding that everything in his mind was dominated by his intense conviction of the presence of Christ in his world. The chronicles were compiled in monasteries, but there can be no doubt that the monks who wrote them saw what they were writing as the actors whose deeds they were recording also saw them, with victory and defeat in battle as results to be powerfully affected by prayer, with victory to be thanked for and defeat to be accepted as the inscrutable will of God.

We cannot tell how much Alfred's grandfather, Egbert, had been influenced by his stay as a young man at the Court of Charlemagne, when Charlemagne was at the height of his great power and prestige. After his coronation, Charlemagne was meant to succeed to the Western half of the Roman Empire. It had been no novelty, even before the conversion of Constantine, that there should be two Emperors, one based on Italy and one on the Bosphorus, so vast were the frontiers to be guarded, the territories to be governed. Britain had been part of that Roman Empire, and some of the Northumbrian kings accepted, in name at least, the overlordship of Charlemagne, but the most important king in England, Offa of Mercia, although he corresponded with Charlemagne and traded with him, refused any formal link or acknowledgment that his domains were part of the revived Roman Empire. The kings of Wessex, at that time much under Mercian influence, took the same position.

Nevertheless, when Ethelwulf's journey to Rome took him through a succession of Carolingian territories, he was accorded courteous welcome and, for part of the journey, an armed escort. On the return journey, Ethelwulf and Alfred stayed for some time at the Court of Charlemagne's grandson, Charles the Bald, who had inherited the lands destined to become France, and there Ethelwulf was accepted by Charles as a son-in-law. Ethelwulf was no longer young, and had grown-up sons who were older than his young bride, Judith, and it seems probable that he was accepted because Charles hoped to bring Wessex to acknowledge him, however vaguely, as overlord.

The marriage ceremony took place in October after a betrothal ceremony in July. The rite was performed by Hincmar of Rheims, a man famous in his day and a champion of Judgment by Ordeal as against his more enlightened contemporary Agobard of Lyons. During nuptial Mass, just before the Gospel, the Archbishop put a ring on Judith's finger, told

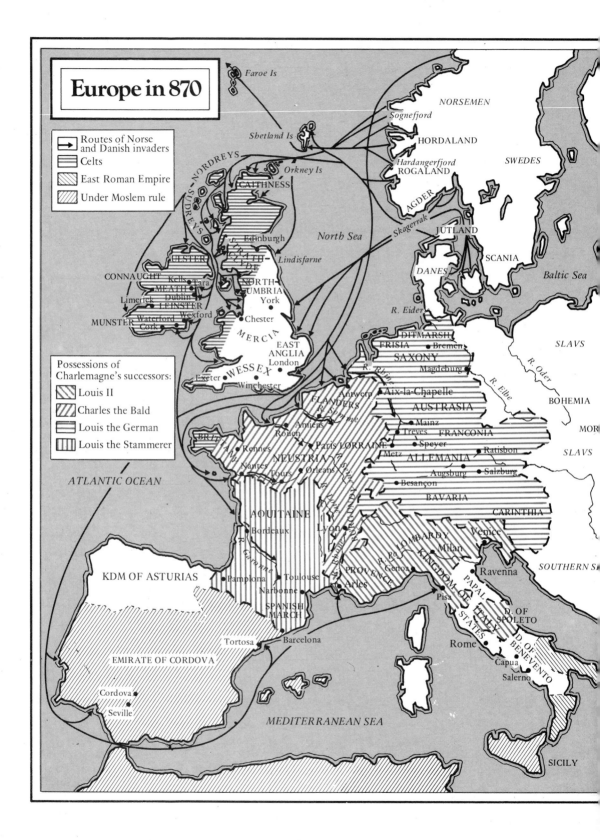

Europe in 870

Legend:
- → Routes of Norse and Danish invaders
- Celts
- East Roman Empire
- Under Moslem rule

Possessions of Charlemagne's successors:
- Louis II
- Charles the Bald
- Louis the German
- Louis the Stammerer

Faroe Is

NORSEMEN

Sognefjord

HORDALAND

SWEDES

Shetland Is

Hardangerfjord
ROGALAND

Orkney Is

NORDREYS

CAITHNESS

AGDER

Skagerrak

JUTLAND

North Sea

SCANIA

SUDREYS

Edinburgh

Lindisfarne

DANES

Baltic Sea

ULSTER

CONNAUGHT
Kells Tara

MEATH Dublin

Limerick LEINSTER

MUNSTER Waterford Wexford

Cork

Chester

NORTH-
UMBRIA
York

R. Eider

DITMARSH

FRISIA Bremen

SLAVS

R. Oder

MERCIA

EAST
ANGLIA
London

SAXONY

Magdeburg

R. Rhine

R. Elbe

BOHEMIA

Exeter WESSEX
Winchester

FLANDERS
R. Seyme
Antwerp

Aix-la-Chapelle

AUSTRASIA

Mainz

FRANCONIA

MOR

ATLANTIC OCEAN

BRIT.

Rennes

Amiens
Rouen

Paris LORRAINE

Treves

Speyer

Metz

ALLEMANIA

Ratisbon

SLAVS

Nantes

NEUSTRIA

Orleans

Augsburg Salzburg

Tours

Besançon

BAVARIA

AQUITAINE

Lyon

CARINTHIA

Bordeaux

R. Garonne

R. Rhone

LOMBARDY

Milan

Venice

KDM OF ASTURIAS

Pamplona

Toulouse

PROVENCE

Po

Genoa

Ravenna

Narbonne

Arles

Pisa

PAPAL

SOUTHERN S

SPANISH
MARCH

KINGDOM OF ITALY

STATES

D. OF
SPOLETO

Tortosa Barcelona

Rome

D. OF
BENEVENTO

EMIRATE OF CORDOVA

Capua

Cordova

Salerno

Seville

MEDITERRANEAN SEA

SICILY

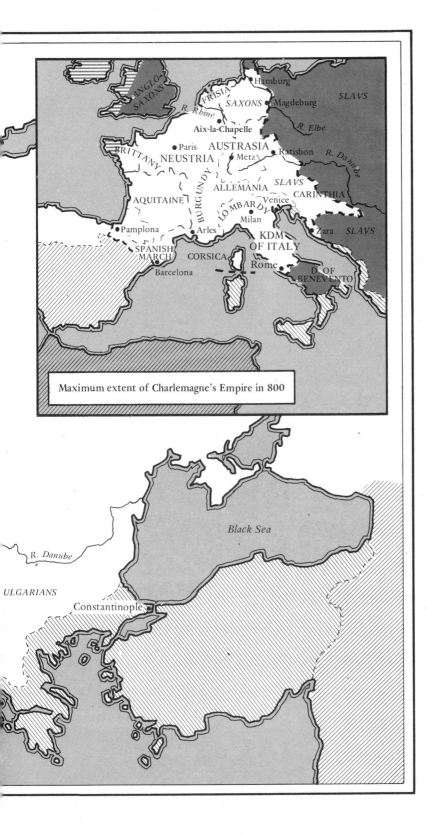

Maximum extent of Charlemagne's Empire in 800

her she was now wedded to the kingdom and then anointed her on the head and placed a crown there. Perhaps Charles the Bald knew that in Wessex queens were not crowned and could not rule as they had among the Merovingians, and it looks very much as though the Carolingian king had designs through his daughter to bring Wessex into his control.

When we come to the Danish wars in the next chapter, it will be seen that unity of command in the West (such as Ethelwulf's link with Charles of France might have brought) would have been invaluable against the same enemy who alternately sailed up the Thames or the Seine. The movements of the Danes on the mainland of Europe were closely watched from England, but there is no indication of how the intelligence was collected or transmitted. But there was a realisation that it was of the first importance because when the Danes were checked in any part of England, they went back to the Continent. Many of them probably set out not from Scandinavia but from what is now Schleswig-Holstein, or from Jutland and Frisia, and we are expressly told that when Alfred was building up his fleet, he secured seamen from Frisia, the very part of the Carolingian Empire in which Charlemagne's son, Louis the Pious, had invited some Vikings to settle, and where they had settled without being cured of their marauding and plundering ways.

From Ethelwulf's second marriage we must infer that Alfred's mother had died, and it may very well be that it was her death that made Ethelwulf finally leave for Rome. Alfred's mother, Osburh by name, was renowned for her piety, but we get only one glimpse of her when Asser tells how she showed an illuminated book of Saxon poems to her sons, and said she would give it to whichever of them could learn to read it first; Alfred was much more eager than his elder brothers, found someone to teach him how to read it aloud and triumphantly carried off the prize. This could not have been Judith, who was a little girl of fourteen, younger than her husband's elder sons, and not being a Saxon herself, but a Frank, is unlikely to have been fond of Saxon poetry. The dates of the story present some difficulties which are best resolved by placing it after Alfred's return from Rome for the first time and before he set out with his father on the second visit. This would place it in the year 854, when he was five or six.

OPPOSITE Charles the Bald, grandson of Charlemagne, who ruled the lands that were to become France. His daughter Judith became Alfred's stepmother.

41

Silver pennies of Alfred's father, Ethelwulf (right), struck at Winchester c. 840, and of his brother, Ethelbert (opposite), made at Canterbury c. 865.

These three episodes, the book of poems and the two visits to Rome, are the three landmarks about which we learn from Asser. Otherwise, Alfred has no place in history till he emerges as a young man of twenty by the side of his third brother, Ethelred.

When Ethelwulf returned from Rome, his second son, who ruled in Kent, seems to have relinquished his authority to his father readily enough, but the eldest son, Ethelbald, was unwilling to do so, and was supported by one of the two chief bishops of Wessex, the Bishop of Sherborne. It was not at all unnatural for sons to be associated with their fathers in government, and Ethelwulf himself had ruled under Egbert. Ethelwulf was probably in failing health, for he died eleven months after his return from Rome, and he made no effort to displace his eldest son from the government of the western half of the Wessex kingdom. When he died, that son, Ethelbald, promptly married the young widow, Judith, a proceeding that caused

42

much scandal as being within the canonically forbidden degree. Ethelbald survived his father by only a little over three years; the *Chronicle* says little about him, and Asser only that his rule was unbridled, which may well be a reference to the scandalous marriage and to nothing more. There then follows, from 862 to 866, the reign of the second son, Ethelbert, in which, as will be related in the next chapter, the Danish invasions became more menacing than ever.

From the story of the book of Saxon poems, we may conclude that Alfred's elder brothers were either very good-natured or not very interested that they allowed their young brother to carry it off, learn it by heart and win it apparently without any competition. This studious disposition, although his father seems to have shared it, set him apart, but it did not mean that he was any less fond of the great outdoor sports of the nobility, hunting, shooting and fishing, although in those days the shooting was done as part of the hunting, with arrows fired

RIGHT The Frank's casket, a whalebone box
made in Northumbria in the early eighth
century, is a magnificent example of
Anglo-Saxon craftsmanship. The casket is
carved in a variety of pagan, classical and
Christian scenes, decorated with traditional
motifs and inscribed with Northumbrian
runes. The side illustrated below shows
soldiers carrying spears and shepherds
with crooks.

from the saddle. He kept up his hunting, at any rate, until he was forty, and in all probability, longer. He was only fifty when he died, and it was only because he had promulgated laws that later representations show him as an old man with a long white beard. We should think of him as clean-shaven, as the crude silver pennies depict him, with a very large chin which may just have been the designer's lack of skill, though it is not inappropriate if it is meant to show strength of will, for Alfred was a man of exceptional resolution and self-discipline.

There seems no question that he suffered nearly all his life from ill-health, from some sort of complaint that was not only painful and chronic but humiliating. Asser tells us that as a youth he was afraid that this would make him unfit to play a leading part as a king's son should, even a younger son. For although he cannot have anticipated that all his brothers would die, he could expect, according to the custom of his family, that he would rule under his father or brother in some part of Wessex, very likely the ancient kingdom of Kent, for which his Jutish blood from his mother would have made him particularly suitable. So he prayed to be relieved of his infirmity, but also that God would send him some other infirmity. It seems probable that here Asser is setting down what the King himself had told him, that the prayer was heard, and the first form of sickness left him, but that when he was nineteen, and at his wedding festivities, another affliction came upon him and remained with him for the next twenty years. It seems vain to conjecture what either illness was, but there can be no reason for doubting the substantial truth that he suffered from ill-health, for it was not a matter of which anyone would boast. Indeed, it was widely attributed – as by Asser – as a punishment for wrong-doing, a disregard for justice in his first years of authority, and physical incapacity was quickly seized upon among the ruling families in Europe as grounds for disqualifying a man from the throne. It did not prevent Alfred from being an outstanding warrior, engaging in hand-to-hand fighting, charging uphill against the Danes in his first campaign, and what is perhaps even more remarkable, it did not make him testy and ill-tempered. One of the chief characteristics that struck Asser was Alfred's extraordinary cheerfulness and affability, and his generosity towards all the individuals who had recourse to him.

We are so dependent for any detailed knowledge of Alfred on Asser's eye-witness account, that it is necessary to form an impression of Asser himself. He came from Pembrokeshire, a part of South Wales which was later to be extensively colonised from England in a way that has always marked it off from the rest of Wales, but at this time it was thoroughly Welsh. Although Saxons from Mercia had made settlements in Glamorgan, and Tenby is a Danish place-name, the great earthwork known as Offa's Dyke is the most tangible evidence that the Saxons recognised a frontier. When Asser was invited to join Alfred's Court, it was part of the general policy in which Alfred emulated Charlemagne, as he did in so many matters, of inviting learned men from outside his own dominions because there were not enough to be found at home.

The practice of obtaining skilled literary help from the richer resources of the Continent, which was to be so marked a feature of Alfred's reign, did not originate with him. His father, Ethelwulf, had a Frank called Felix who was his secretary for some years, and he was the friend of Abbot Lupus of Ferrières near Etaple, who had himself been educated by one of Alcuin's monks. There still exists the begging letter which Lupus wrote to Ethelwulf in which, after many compliments and good wishes for Ethelwulf's eternal well-being, he came to the point of the letter, a request to Ethelwulf to contribute towards covering the abbey church at Ferrières with lead. From a letter Lupus wrote to Felix at the same time, urging him to keep Ethelwulf up to the mark, it is clear Lupus was hoping not for a money contribution but for the lead itself to be sent to Etaple.

Asser has left us a detailed account of how he first came to know Alfred, then residing near Chichester at East Dene. (Alfred seems to have spent a good deal of time in Sussex, and Alfriston, in the east of the county, commemorates this. It makes very good sense to think that when he was engaged on building a new kind of ship, bigger and faster than the Viking ships they were meant to intercept, he resided near the coast, and that the building took place in and around the Solent, Portsmouth and perhaps Bosham Harbour.) What Alfred sought from Asser, as from the other learned clerics whose presence he secured, was someone who would read to him and talk with him on serious intellectual and religious themes. He

47

OPPOSITE A section of Offa's Dyke near Llanfair in Shropshire, looking north west. The dyke was built from the Dee estuary to the Bristol Channel by King Offa of Mercia in the second half of the eighth century to mark a firm boundary between his kingdom and Wales.

never ceased to deplore his own lack of education, and Asser, while praising the deep piety of Alfred's parents, makes a sharp criticism of their failure to do as much as they might for their brilliant son's early education. This seems unfair if it is accepted that his mother must have died before his second visit to Rome, which ended in his father returning with a young second wife from the Frankish Court, and Ethelwulf himself died a year later when Alfred was not more than eleven years old. It is much more probable that it was because he was thus orphaned and then lived with elder brothers who did not share his thirst for education, that his progress was slow, and that his loud and constant lament about his own deficiencies was rather parallel to the declarations of spiritual unworthiness which come heartfelt from men who have caught a glimpse of real spirituality. Alfred became aware that he was living in an age of rapid intellectual decline, and that whereas on the battlefield he was well-equipped, he was ill-equipped for the equally uphill task of reviving learning. He made these remarks to men more learned than himself, quite genuinely, but also because he was King and had to make it clear that he did not want flatterers or courtiers but teachers. He had, as we shall see, considerable difficulty in both finding and keeping them, but as long as he lived he persevered.

To give the reader a picture of the remarkable man whose fortunes we are to follow, here is how Asser described him in those middle years after the worst struggles with the Danes were over:

Meanwhile amid wars and the frequent hindrances of this present life, the incursions of the Pagans and his own daily infirmities of body, the King did not cease to carry on the government and to engage in hunting of every form; to teach his goldsmiths and all his artificers, his falconers, hawkers and dog-keepers; to erect by his own inventive skill finer and more sumptuous buildings than had ever been the wont of his ancestors; to read aloud Saxon books, and above all, not only to command others to learn Saxon poems by heart but to study them himself in private to the best of his power. He also heard daily the divine office of the mass, with certain psalms and prayers, and celebrated the canonical hours by day and night; and in the night, as we have said, he was wont to frequent the churches for prayer, secretly and without the knowledge of his

Contrasting examples of
Celtic and Anglo-Saxon
metalwork, both of the
eighth century.
LEFT The Athlone Plaque,
a Celtic cast-iron plaque of
the Crucifixion, which
may have been part of a
book cover.
RIGHT Tassilo's chalice,
presented to
Kremsmünster, Austria,
by Tassilo, Duke of
Bavaria, but Anglo-Saxon
in style, probably from
Northumberland. The
fine images of Christ and
the saints make it a work
of great originality, for it
is the only time that
figures appear on a chalice
before the twelfth century.

Hawking, from the October page of a Saxon calendar.

Court. He was a bountiful giver of alms, both to his own countrymen and to foreigners of all nations, incomparably affable and pleasant to all men, and a skilful investigator of the secrets of nature. Many Franks, Frisians, Gauls, Pagans, Britons and Scots, and Armoricans [Bretons] submitted voluntarily to his dominion, both noble and ignoble, all of whom, according to their birth and dignity, he ruled, loved, honoured, and enriched with money and power. He was also wont to listen carefully and attentively to the Holy Scripture read to him by his countrymen, or, if by any chance any came from abroad, to hear prayers in company with foreigners.

52

Moreover, he loved his bishops and the whole order of clergy, his earls and nobles, and all his servants and friends with wonderful affection, and he looked upon their sons, who were brought up in the royal household, as no less dear to him than his own, never ceasing night and day, among other things, to instruct them in all good morals and to teach them letters.

2 The Saving of Wessex

Never before and never since in our history have four brothers succeeded each other on the same throne, and all inside ten years. Ethelbald, Ethelbert and Ethelred were not slain in battle, although they all fought battles, but it is very possible that wounds in battle played their part in cutting short their lives. This seems especially likely to have happened to Ethelred who reigned for five years from 866, the youngest of the three and not more than thirty when he died, for when he was buried at Wimborne it was with special honours as for one who had died for his country and the Christian faith. The House of Cerdic seems to have been generally shortlived, for in the next century three of Alfred's grandsons were to have brief reigns one after the other – Athelstan, Edmund and Edred – and Alfred the Great himself lived only to middle age.

The Alfred who fought the Danes through the seventies was a man in his twenties, who had succeeded to a grim and doubtful inheritance. All his life he had known about the Danes, the pirates who came raiding, looting and burning, going back to their ships and then reappearing up some river or at some other point along the coast. They had appeared in his grandfather Egbert's time, in his father's time and in increasing numbers during the years in which he was growing up to manhood. The year 867 had been particularly memorable for the arrival of an unusually large army under the command of the Danish leader Halfdene which had taken York, and in the succeeding years Mercia and Northumbria were severely ravaged from east to west. The Danes had already started the practice of wintering in England instead of going back to their northern lairs.

For over five hundred years, the provinces of the Roman Empire in western Europe had suffered continual incursions from the north and east, an apparently inexhaustible supply of vigorous and hungry tribes descending on the Empire. Very often an arrangement could be made by which they themselves became, as it were, part of the imperial establishment, poachers turned game-keepers, to hold the frontiers, and such was the awe and prestige of Rome that they were only too proud and satisfied to see themselves as part of the imperial ruling class. But there were great differences between the tribes. There were some who moved in large numbers, seeking the great cities where there was most wealth to be collected, and

PREVIOUS PAGES
An Anglo-Saxon
battle scene.

OPPOSITE A Valkyrie, one
of the fierce warrior
maidens who served the
god Odin, from an
eighth-century picture
stone in Gotland, Sweden.

56

moving on, often leaving no lasting trace of their presence. Such were the Alains and Vandals who are believed to have ended up in North Africa and mingled their blood with other inhabitants, to create the Berbers. There were other tribes who sought land to settle on, and to divide up into separate families, the tribes out of whom the feudal system was to arise by which such land was given to individuals in return for military service; both the Saxons and the Danes belonged to this grouping.

At the beginning of this century, the French historian Henri de Tourville developed the theory that the decisive experience which differentiated one group of northern tribes from the other took place in Norway. He argued that these tribes, coming from the steppes in the east and moving all the time westward, had gone into Scandinavia. Gothland, indeed, is a placename in Sweden, and the title of the Swedish royal House calls the king 'King of the Swedes and Goths'. But there was nothing decisive about the geography of Sweden, with its large area and open country. It was in Norway that the tribes had to split up. They found a country full of fjords with deep water, protected by a shelf of rock rich in fish, but suited only for small fishing vessels, with a little land where families could settle but not whole tribes. Because these farms could provide a living for only one family, the younger sons had to leave and seek their fortune and, as it were, band themselves together to go back to the old tribal life, to go abroad and seek and win for themselves first wealth and eventually land, where they too could take root and found their families. The way to do this was to get accepted into a war band, and these varied very much in quality according to the leadership. There were what might be called crack regiments (except that regiments suggest some-thing much larger), where men had to pass tests to prove their physical strength and endurance, such as lifting an immensely heavy stone. For the man who could not stand up to the priva-tions of the sea journey and then at the end of it be ready to fight, was a liability, and there was no room for passengers in the Viking ships. Although the latter had a large square sail, they also relied on the oars which the fighting men were not too proud to use. They had no mariners' compass, and the northern seas could be very rough. They used to take birds and release them and follow their flight, knowing it would lead sooner or

OPPOSITE A Viking ship, showing the customary square sail, from an eighth-century picture stone.

59

later to land, but some of them wandered out far into the Atlantic, and some even reached the North American continent.

But the general instinct was to turn south, to look for the rivers, to find the Rhine and the Meuse and the Seine and the Loire; some ships even found their way into the Mediterranean and came up by the east coast of Spain to the south of France. It is related that the Emperor Charlemagne, as early as 794, was filled with apprehension when the news was brought to him that these northern pirates had found the southern route. Now Europe throughout the ninth century would be exposed to constant attack, both from the north and from the south, from Danes and Saracens, and the great rivers which with their tributaries made the land fertile, and along whose banks towns large and small were growing up as commerce directed, would become a great source of military weakness.

Wessex had one great advantage over Mercia, that it was separated by the Bristol Channel from the Welsh. Offa of Mercia had built Offa's Dyke, a kind of western equivalent of the Roman Wall that was meant to protect Northumbria, but the Welsh were numerous and formidable enemies, whereas the Celts in Cornwall lived on the defensive. The two kingdoms of Mercia and Wessex had continual intermarriage between their royal Houses (Alfred married Elswitha of Mercia) and both Ethelwulf and his son Ethelred went to the help of Mercia when appealed to for aid against the Welsh or the Danes. Alfred's first appearance in military history is in 868 when as a youth not quite twenty he accompanied his elder brother Ethelred to help the Mercians dislodge the Danes from Nottingham. They were unsuccessful because the Danes had fortified themselves behind a stockade, and this defence, though consisting only of deep ditches and wooden stakes, gave the defenders a great advantage.

The importance of these stockades shows how very primitive the fighting was. There was little cavalry, though the Danes stole horses when they could. The Saxons fought on foot, and the axe with which Alfred's statues at Winchester and Wantage depict him was a formidable all-purpose weapon with which a man could hew his way through a stockade and reach his armoured enemy, whose armour could better withstand a sword than an axe. But the swords were lighter, quicker to use,

The two sides of a silver penny of King Ethelred of Wessex struck by a moneyer Ethered *c.* 870, probably from the Canterbury mint. It was found with many others of the same period at Beeston Tor, Derbyshire.

equally indispensable, and there were spears and bows and arrows. Neither side had even primitive stone-throwing artillery, the *ballista* which the Romans and other peoples of antiquity had used, which could have been most effective against stockades. No doubt the strength of a stockade, such as Alfred himself built at Athelney at the lowest point of his fortunes, pointed the way to one of his great strategic improvements, the institution of *burhs* or fortified mounds at key points all over his kingdom.

Man for man, the pirate Danes, whose sole occupation was war, were more than a match for most of the peasants who answered the call of their county's *ealdormen* or their thanes, and came bravely to the field with such weapons as they had: some sort of shield, if only of wood, but perhaps a trophy taken from a slain enemy at an earlier fight; a spear, a sword, a dagger, a bow. The thanes were better armed and probably as heavily protected as their leading enemies. Sometimes the Roman *testudo* or tortoise formation seems to have been used. This meant that a group of men, each with his shield above his head, horizontal and interlocking with the shields of his companions, advanced slowly towards the enemy, virtually immune to the arrows that might rain upon them before they could close with their foes. The weakness of the Danes was that they needed to forage for plunder and food, increasingly far afield from their base, and if the Saxon leaders had good information and a strategic reserve, they could intercept and overwhelm them by superior numbers. The carnage was bloody, for no prisoners were taken, and many Danes must have lost their lives over-encumbered with plunder. Most of the engagements were in the open, with the enemies seeking each other out because they had little in the way of supplies. In addition to those killed outright, we have to envisage many mortally wounded and left to die later of their wounds, in an age of primitive medicine.

When Alfred began to reign, no answer had been found to the Danish onslaught beyond the building here and there of high watchtowers like those which still stand, as at Arbroath on the east coast of Scotland or on the east coast of Ireland, but they were not known in the south. From these high towers or equally high cliffs, several hours of warning could be obtained for people to leave their farmsteads and hide, or perhaps, if the

OPPOSITE The round tower at Clonmacnois, County Offaly, Eire, from which a look-out was kept for Viking raiders. In the foreground is a tenth-century Celtic cross.

63

Saxon and Viking weapons

Although the sword was the most important weapon of the time, it has not been found in graves as frequently as other weapons, possibly because swords were precious objects, handed down from father to son and believed to gain virtue with age.

BELOW The hilt of a Saxon sword.
RIGHT A Viking sword.
BOTTOM The bronze hilt from a Viking sword.

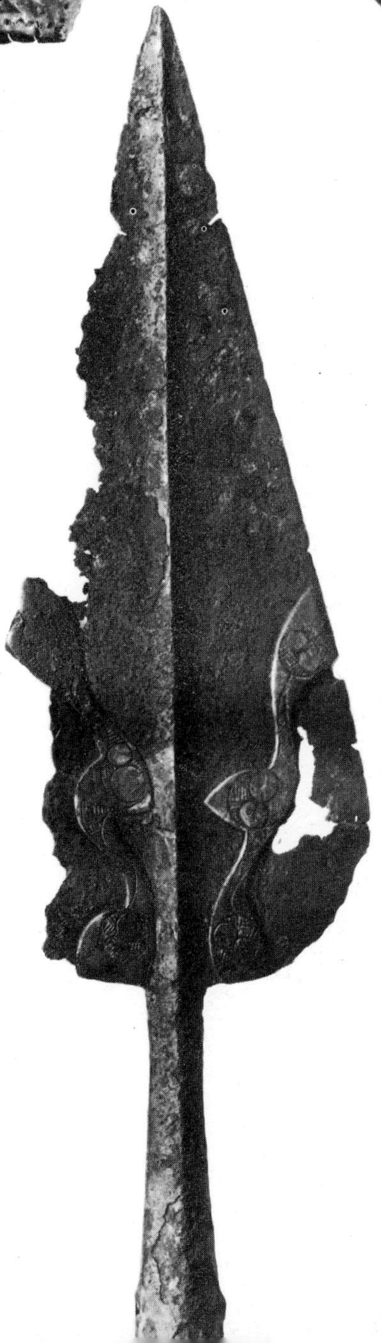

Three weapons found in
various places along the
River Thames:
ABOVE A Viking battle
axe found near
London Bridge.
FAR LEFT An iron
spearhead from Dachet.
LEFT A late-Saxon knife
found by Wandsworth.

raiders were few, to organise resistance. The Carolingian Empire was no more successful than were the inhabitants of the British Isles until Alfred showed how real defence could be organised.

The reign of Ethelred had been a time of respite for Wessex. The Danes were busy in the north of England, taking York in 867, and in East Anglia, where in 870 they had murdered the King, Edmund, who refused to become their subject and was regarded as a martyr, and whose tomb at Bury St Edmunds and the great abbey built round it have ensured his lasting fame. But in the year 871, when Alfred succeeded to the throne, Wessex felt the full fury of the Danes. Coming up the Thames, they entrenched themselves at the junction of the Kennet and the Thames on the spur of land protected on two sides by water, where the great abbey of Reading was one day to be built by Henry I, the Norman king who married a descendant of Alfred, a daughter of St Margaret of Scotland. The royal brothers attacked the Danes at Reading and were repulsed from the Danish stockade. The men of Berkshire under their *ealdormen* intercepted and defeated a Danish party at Englefield, six miles north-west of Reading. Then there follows the last victory of Ethelred's reign, the battle of Ashdown.

The battle of Ashdown has been remembered beyond its strategic importance. It was fought a few days after Ethelred and Alfred had been repulsed at Reading, which suggests that the Danes were seeking to follow up their advantage. It was fought at the extreme west end of the Berkshire Downs, where White Horse Hill rises to eight hundred feet. The northern escarpment on which the White Horse is cut in the chalk drops steeply and overlooks the Vale of White Horse. But to the south, the land slopes away more gradually from the brow of the hill where stands Uffington Castle. This is a most impressive earthwork, generally dated long before the Roman occupation and belonging to the Iron Age. Its sides are precipitous and its ditches deep. Yet we are told in the *Chronicle* that the Danes occupied the high ground where one would have expected the Saxons; that they moved out to meet the Saxons, and that the fiercest fighting took place south of Uffington Castle by a tree that was shown for centuries. It is a puzzling battle, for the *Chronicle* says that the Danes were in two armies, one under two of their kings and the other under an unspecified number of *jarls*, who may be taken as corresponding to Saxon *ealdormen*, commanders of proved worth but not royal. Ethelred was to attack the kings, Alfred the *jarls*. Alfred told Asser that when the Danes were moving and he went to fetch his brother, Ethelred was hearing Mass, and insisted on waiting till the Mass was ended. This does not seem to have affected the course of the battle, which proved to be a complete Saxon victory. One of the two kings, Bagsecg, was slain, but the *jarls* lost five of their number, including two called Sidroc, apparently additional to the Sidroc who, we are told, was killed at Englefield. But this great victory was inconclusive. Two days later the two sides were engaged in combat again at Basing, and this time the Danes had the better of it. It was for a long time thought that the White Horse had been cut to commemorate Alfred's victory, but it is now agreed that it is far older. It is more like a greyhound than a horse, 325 feet long, and there is a coin, Romano-British or earlier, with a figure very like it.

Later in 871 King Ethelred died of battle wounds and although he left children, Alfred was immediately recognised as capable of defending the land. In fact, the year's campaign fizzled out. The Danes penetrated deep into Wiltshire and were victorious at Wilton, but nothing serious seems to have followed. Although the *Chronicle* often talks of great slaughter, it seems clear that the numbers on each side should probably be reckoned in hundreds, and that the fighting men living this very hard life of march and counter-march and chance provisions, cannot have cared for the seriously wounded, had no fixed lines of communication and were so exhausted that both sides were ready for a truce before the winter set in. It was not a very glorious opening to Alfred's reign in spite of the spectacular victory at Ashdown. The kind of truce he made has many parallels elsewhere. It was an agreement that in return for a payment the Danes would withdraw from his part of the island, but it left them quite free to try their fortune elsewhere. They retreated down the Thames to London which they had taken from the Mercians, and there are still in existence in the British Museum silver pennies struck in London by the Danish leader Halfdene, who had fought at Ashdown. These coins, similar to Saxon silver pennies, show the firm hold the Danes

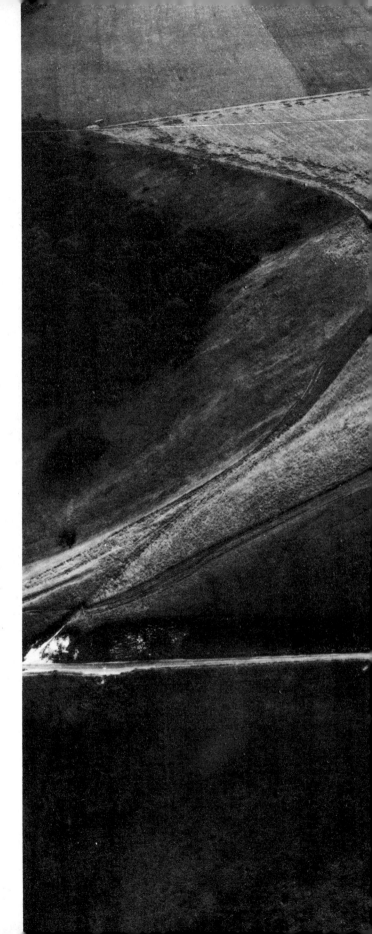

The Uffington White
Horse marks the site of
Ethelred's and Alfred's
victory over the Danes at
the battle of Ashdown, but
it was cut centuries before.

68

had and their expectation that they could maintain it. Wessex had a respite, but only because the Danes turned their raids north-east and north-west, went back into East Anglia and Mercia, and in Mercia were so successful that Alfred's brother-in-law, King Burghred, was driven from the kingdom, and took refuge in Rome, while the Danes set up what today we should call a Quisling government, with a Mercian noble, Coelwulf. Already we can see in the early seventies the shape of the great settlement by which England was later to be divided along the line of Watling Street from London to Chester, with all to the north of it conceded for Danish settlement, and all south of it, mainly Wessex and west Mercia, being closed to them.

There was then an uneasy lull, for Alfred had only done what so many other local rulers had done, persuaded the Danes to ravage somewhere else. They resumed their depredations not only in East Anglia but in Mercia, and it seems reasonably clear that Alfred took an active part in Mercia against the puppet Saxon king Coelwulf. It seems very probable that it was because Wessex was the support and strength of the Saxon

A silver penny struck by the Danish leader Halfdene with a monogram of LONDONIA on one side.

opposition to the Danes in Mercia that the Danes, for their part, concluded that it would be necessary, if they were to keep their hold in Mercia, to break the power of Wessex. The fact of Halfdene's minting coins in London, which had been under Mercian rule for so long, suggests very strongly that the Danes hoped and believed they had secured not only control of the north in York, but control of East Anglia and Mercia, and that if only they could reduce Wessex to the same subjection, they could make themselves the dominant caste (just as some two hundred years later their frenchified cousins the Northmen of Normandy were to succeed in doing under William the Conqueror). With Burghred in exile in Rome, the leadership of the Saxons in Mercia passed to an *ealdorman*, Ethelred, a valiant warrior, to whom Alfred later gave one of his daughters in marriage. She was to earn an honourable place for herself in the next reign as the Lady of the Mercians.

The fundamental strength of Wessex, by contrast with Northumbria and Mercia, was that only its northern frontier was a land frontier and, if it could command the sea, it was strategically and commercially the most advantageously situ-

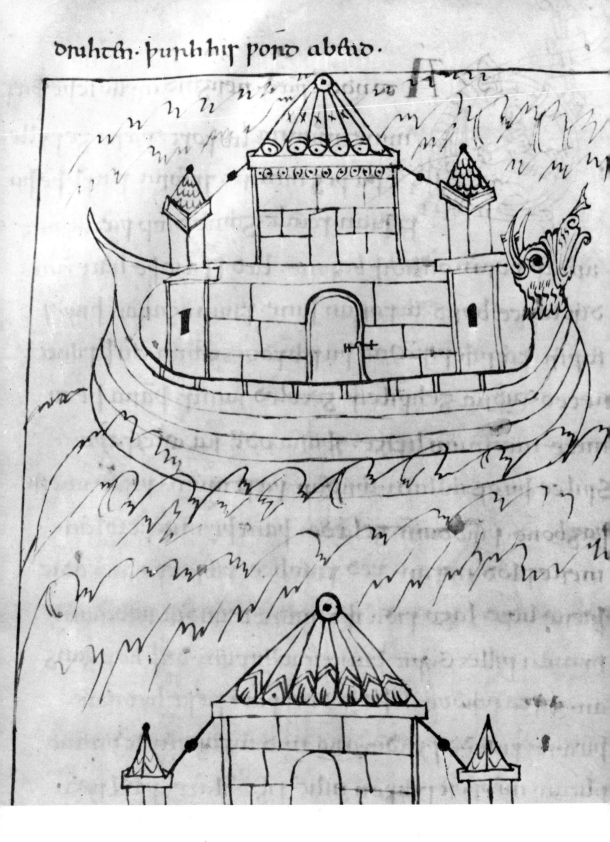

ated part of the British Isles. Although Alfred earned the title 'Father of the Royal Navy', when he undertook the building of ships to intercept the Danes, he was not the first King of Wessex to do so. In his father's and grandfather's time, some rudimentary attempts had been made to meet the pirates, as *The Anglo-Saxon Chronicle* constantly calls them, before they landed. Then they were in a relatively defenceless position, crowded in their long, narrow boats which could be sunk if they could be rammed, and which were very difficult to manœuvre by sail; while the oars were out, those using them could be shot at with arrows. There were one or two small naval successes of this kind, but it was Alfred who first appreciated the importance for the Saxons of building numerous vessels and training men to be at least as competent as the Danes in handling them.

However, there was more to the survival of Wessex than its geographical position. The fate of East Anglia shows how a long sea-frontier could be vulnerable and although the East Anglians were in a particularly exposed position, occupying the nearest shores to the Danes, it also seems clear that they lacked the sustained military vigour which helped the West Saxons maintain their independence. Except for one brief period in the middle seventies, which may be called Alfred's Second Danish War, the Danes never got their claws into Wessex as tenaciously as they did in the other kingdoms.

As the sequel was to show in the next century, if the Danes could not conquer Wessex they would lose Mercia, and this gave sufficient reason for the all-out effort that they made in the middle of the late seventies against Wessex. The attack was concerted by both land and sea, and the march southward was supported, though the chronology is a little uncertain, by the landing of a large fleet which took possession of Wareham in the east of Dorset. The chronicler tells us that many of the people of Hampshire fled overseas. This must have been a hazardous enterprise, only undertaken because the alternative seemed to be death at the hands of the invaders. Of these flights from Wessex some interpreters argue that in the west of the kingdom 'overseas' could mean the Bristol Channel, but the Danes were strongly entrenched at the mouth of the Severn on both sides of the river and in Glamorgan. They never raided Brittany, and it seems probable that anyone who fled from

OPPOSITE Noah's Ark from a tenth-century manuscript illustrating Genesis by means of contemporary scenes. The hull of the ship is similar to those built for Alfred's navy.

73

Viking ships

The excavation of a ship at Oseberg, Norway (opposite below), revealed the great skill of the Scandanavian shipbuilders who, using only pine-root pegs to hold the ship together, were able to shape and fit the narrow planking of the hull for speed, strength and watertightness. The reconstructed prow (right) is a masterpiece of Viking art; the craftsman carved lines of interlaced animal forms ending in a serpent's head. The ship had been the burial place of a princess whose body lay in the centre surrounded by sacrificed animals.

LEFT A reconstruction of a ship found at Gokstad, Norway. The ship is 72 feet long with a beam of 17 feet and a draught of only 3 feet. The planks at the base are less than one inch thick yet were able to withstand the battering of the Atlantic waves.

Hampshire overseas had no choice but to go south into France, to the country that the Northmen were so shortly to make their own as Normandy.

Though we learn from the *Chronicle* of a disaster to a group of Danish ships dashed against the coast at Purbeck, in the main they seem to have selected and reached Exeter, to make it into a base for their operations in the western half of Wessex. Exeter was an important town with the episcopal see of Crediton ten miles away (from which St Boniface had gone a century and a half before to become the apostle of North Germany, and to be martyred in lands in which the Northmen had now settled, the coasts and islands of Frisia). The sea disaster off Purbeck and Swanage had involved 120 ships, perhaps something like five thousand fighting men, allowing forty to a ship. Nevertheless, there were enough Danes in Exeter to put up a resistance through the summer months of 877, but it remains a puzzle why both at Wareham and at Exeter, having run such hazards to establish themselves in such strategically advantageous positions, they then agreed in each instance to make peace and depart when resolutely confronted, as Alfred did confront them. They gave hostages and swore their solemn heathen oaths, the most solemn being an oath on the holy ring, which was a ring placed on the heathen altar and reddened with the blood of a sacrificed animal. But the record shows that for all the solemnity of this oath-taking, it weighed very lightly with the Danes if they could suddenly perceive some short-term advantage in breaking it, and the peace they made at Exeter, followed by a withdrawal into Mercia, lasted just five months, until the beginning of 878.

The Wessex kings had a royal *vill* at Chippenham as they had at Wantage and Faringdon and many other places. It is reasonable to suppose that a royal *vill* prepared to entertain the king and his companions in some modest state, had good farmsteads and produce and was a fairly grand manorial estate, and as such was full of attractive booty. Under Guthrum, the Danish leader who now appears prominently on the scene, a surprise descent on Chippenham, at the end of the Twelve Days of Christmas festivities, was completely successful. We are left in the dark why it was that Alfred, whose military intelligence was generally good and who even managed to keep a close watch on the movements of Danish ships and armies on the mainland of Europe and the territories nearest to Wessex, and who had been not unsuccessful across the borders in Mercia, was taken completely by surprise. It may have been partly because the Danes did not, as they usually did, wait until the spring weather, but perhaps also because they had been so very emphatic at Exeter, offering him all the hostages he cared to take. Whatever the explanation, the onslaught seems to have been overwhelming. Wessex had no immediate answer, and there began the lowest period in Alfred's personal fortunes. He was driven into Somerset, to the island of Athelney, where in March, in the water-logged land, he created a stockaded fortress and began to seek to organise an effective counter-attack. It may well be that Alfred chose Athelney because he wanted to be within easy reach of Exeter in case the Danes reappeared there, for Athelney is roughly equidistant between Exeter and Chippenham. (To-day Athelney would not strike anybody as an island, but in the ninth century Somerset was far more water-logged, undrained and uncultivated, and to this circumstance may be attributed the immunity of Glastonbury Abbey from the fate which overtook so many other monasteries, of being sacked and ravaged and their monks murdered by the Danes, like Abingdon Abbey which took a century to recover.)

To this period belongs the famous story of the cakes, by which alone Alfred is remembered by so many of his fellow-countrymen. The story is that he was so preoccupied with his military problems, and even with mending his own modest weapons, that when asked by the herdsman's wife with whom he had taken shelter, to watch the cakes that were being baked, he forgot about them and they were badly burned. Not knowing who he was, she angrily upbraided him, but he is said to have accepted her scolding with meakness. The story is first found in a twelfth-century life of St Neot, who is believed to have been King Alfred's kinsman, perhaps his half-brother, but Queen Elizabeth I's Archbishop of Canterbury, Matthew Parker (to whom we owe so much for his care in rescuing and saving copies of the *Anglo-Saxon Chronicle* when there was so much wanton destruction of anything medieval), in editing Asser's *Life of Alfred*, inserted the anecdote there, from which it was copied into successive histories. It is an anecdote which,

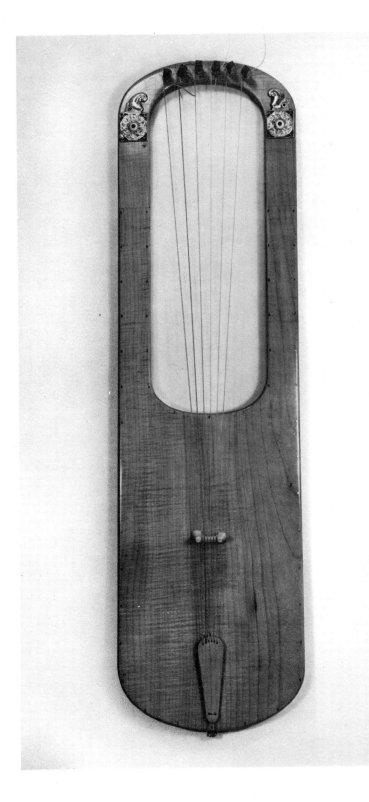

An Anglo-Saxon lyre
reconstructed from pieces
found at the Sutton Hoo
ship burial.

whether historical or not, has nothing improbable about it, for it illustrates the wretchedness to which the Wessex dynasty had been reduced.

After the chronicler has told us of the demoralisation of the Saxons, we realise that it cannot have been more than a temporary panic for the *ealdormen* of Hampshire and Wiltshire were able to collect bodies of men and to meet Alfred at a place which has defied identification, the *Chronicle* calling it 'Egbert's Stone'. Naturally this would suggest Kingston-upon-Thames in the east of the kingdom, because that is where Egbert had been crowned and had started the practice which nearly all his successors followed, of being crowned on the king's stone at the riverside town. But this seems a highly improbable *rendezvous* for Alfred to have assigned to his supporters when he was himself in the middle of Somerset, gathering an army to drive the Danes back into Mercia from their stronghold at Chippenham. In fact, the chroniclers tell us that Egbert's Stone was at the east end of Penselwood, which with Selwood formed a natural protection of woodland near the Somerset–Wiltshire borders. At this meeting, the levies from Somerset and Wiltshire were reinforced from Hampshire. We are told that even when he had no forces but the local Somerset levies, Alfred continually went over to the offensive and harried the Danes, and it may well be to this period that there should be credited the tradition that he himself, disguised as a wandering minstrel, went into one of the Danish camps to entertain them and pick up information. It is a story which is not found before the fourteenth century, and it has been treated sceptically because so prudent a commander, well aware how vital his own presence and personality were to the Saxon resistance, is unlikely to have taken so foolhardy a risk of being treated as a Saxon spy, even if he was not obviously someone of superior rank.

As soon as Alfred had the combined forces at his disposal, he set out towards Chippenham. The Danes met him on the Wiltshire downs at Ethandune near the village of Edington. After a long day's fighting, the Saxons won a victory which proved decisive. The Danes were pursued to Chippenham and there besieged, and after ten days, instead of trying to break out, sued for peace, offering all the hostages Alfred chose to demand. We are told that the Danes were reduced to privation

ABOVE The White Horse near Westbury, Wiltshire, may have been carved
to commemorate Alfred's victory over the Danes at Ethandune. It is
180 feet long and 107 feet high. It was remodelled in the eighteenth century.

OVERLEAF
Saxon kings with
a prisoner.

81

Đa dīc bæhīsr hū rūm man · M
bpodon rūnu · onbīmdum
damaíce̸· Nobilif ur̄bf fenicif · Eodē aū uoc
pouro maíech ꝫ libi uelīc ĩlubrīf · hēbu
nīr̄pīf sum fund̄c · Ohcioꝫ ñ ꝗ ancillā al

τ ꞃæꝺe abꝡaꞃꞃꞇ huꞅꞃꞇan hyꞃ
læꝺꝺe:

ꝑe maꞅech ancɨlle abꞃaꞃꝁᷓ fɨlɨ² aꝑellaꞇ⁹ ē.
quꞓꞇꞇɨonꞗ plenɨ² dɨꞅꝑꞇꞇauɨꞇ hꞓc canꞇᷓ
e maꞅech, nuncuꝑaꞇᷓ ꝗbemuꞅ᛬

A later copy, translated into Latin in the Quadriparitus *c.* 1114, of the treaty between Alfred and Guthrum of 886. It gave Alfred more territory than the earlier Peace of Wedmore and confirmed his possession of London. It was more an agreement between friendly rulers than conditions imposed by Alfred on a defeated enemy, and accepted the equality in law of Saxons and Danes. Alfred recognised the Danelaw east of Watling Street, provided the Saxons within it were treated fairly.

and despair, which suggests that their considerable encampment must have been totally surrounded, and surrounded in sufficient strength to convince them that an attempt to break out was hopeless. They also promised that their king, Guthrum, and a number of his leading followers would, before they departed northwards, accept baptism, and we are told that Alfred had pity on them, and agreed that he would himself stand sponsor at the font for Guthrum.

Although Chippenham was a Saxon royal *vill*, the ceremony did not take place there, though the Saxons re-possessed themselves of all the booty the Danes had collected and not, as yet, consumed. Then Alfred took Guthrum and thirty of his picked companions all the way back to Athelney. At Aller nearby, the baptism was duly performed. Guthrum received the noble Saxon name of Athelstan. In addition to the baptismal rites of water, he was anointed with chrism and his head bandaged, after which for several days, at another Somerset royal *vill* further north at Wedmore, not far from the Bristol Channel, Alfred entertained him royally and gave him gifts which included houses. It must have been uphill work entertaining the discomforted Northman with a different language and little conversation except military boasting – singularly out of place.

This practice of inviting and insisting on baptism was not original. Charlemagne's son and successor, Louis the Pious, a generation before, had constantly employed it against the Danes, as he also introduced the policy of inviting them to settle in the northern parts of his dominions. Neither policy had justified itself by results. The Danes continued for another half-century to molest the Carolingian Empire, to sail up the Meuse and the Seine and the Somme, and there is a record of one Danish *jarl* complaining grumpily, as he went off to baptism, that this was the twentieth time he had had to go through the ceremony. But that story comes from the mainland, whence Alfred may have derived the idea, which was new in English history although the Danish pirates had been on the island for well over half a century. When they had first appeared at the end of the eighth century, their hatred of the Christian religion (shown when they first sacked Lindisfarne) had been an outstanding characteristic. Probably it was the personality of

Alfred himself, the respect the Danes could not withhold from him as a fighting man, the magnanimity of his spirit, and his deep personal conviction of the truths of Christianity, which made a lasting impression on Guthrum, putting him in a class apart from the other Danish leaders. He kept his pact with Alfred, and it was no doubt by agreement that after a year at Cirencester he moved his army into East Anglia, and began settling them on the land.

The years after Wedmore were not wholly peaceful, but the crisis was past. When a fresh Danish fleet came up the Thames and wintered at Fulham, this did not prove to be the prelude to any attack either north or south of the Thames. We can only surmise that the leaders of this fleet found their hands tied, that Guthrum was in control north of the river and did not want them and that Alfred was too strong to be plundered in the south. They re-crossed the Channel and besieged Ghent, and when another party, coming up the Thames, besieged Rochester, King Alfred marched against them and relieved it. There were one or two sea engagements which suggest that the West Saxons were acquiring skill in seamanship, although on one occasion, after a decisive victory over a small group of Danish ships, the Saxons, laden with booty, had the misfortune to encounter a larger Danish fleet and lost everything, for in these sea engagements if the losers were not drowned, they were killed. There was no room for prisoners in such small boats. In 886 Alfred regained London, and repairing its Roman walls, made it a strong port.

A document exists from the middle eighties which embodies the general terms of settlement, commonly ante-dated to Wedmore and the summer of 878, because it was probably then that the general principle was accepted by which the Saxons agreed to permanent Danish settlements north of the line along the Thames and the Lea, in a straight line to Bedford, up the Ouse to Watling Street and then along it. The document shows the consciousness that the Danes were foreigners, and they were forbidden to settle in the Saxon half of the island, just as Saxons were not to go into what was soon to be called the Danelaw, although of course there were a great many already resident there and occupying the lower places in society. The Danish soldiers who were settled on the land were men with much

RIGHT This font in Deerhurst Church, dating from just after Alfred's death, was probably part of a cross shaft. The spiral motif, very popular in pagan England, was used right up to the Norman Conquest.

87

England at the time of Alfred

The Danelaw

Boundary established by treaty between Alfred and Guthrum, 886

Celts

STRATHCLYDE

Edinburgh

LOTHIAN

R. Tweed

Lindisfarne
Bamburgh

BERNICIA

GALLOWAY Newcastle
Ruthwell

R. Tyne Newcastle

Hexham Jarrow
Monkwearmouth

Carlisle

Durham

Whithorn

R. Tees

NORTHUMBRIA Whitby

Ripon

Isle of Man

IRISH SEA

York

NORTH SEA

Runcorn

R. Trent *R. Humber*

Anglesey Degannwy Chester Bakewell Torksey
Lincoln

GWYNEDD Derby Nottingham *The Wash*

Stafford Repton Crowland North Elmham

Shrewsbury Lichfield Stamford *The Fens* Norwich

Watling Street Leicester Peterborough

Bridgnorth MERCIA Ely EAST ANGLIA

POWYS *R. Severn* Northampton *R. Ouse* Huntingdon Thetford
Dunwich

Worcester Cambridge Bury St Edmunds

Bedford

St Davids Buckingham GUTHRUM'S Colchester
DYFED BRECKNOCK KINGDOM

Offa's Dyke *Wat's Dyke* Gloucester Hertford
Cirencester Oxford Maldon
Ashdown Abingdon *R. Thames* Benfleet

Malmesbury Wantage London *R. Thames*
Bristol Chippenham Reading Kingston Rochester

Wedmore Bath Edington WESSEX Canterbury *Isle of Thanet*
Bradford-on-Avon KENT Dover

Isle of Athelney Sarum Basing
Taunton Glastonbury Wilton Winchester Hastings
Sherborne Romsey
Southampton Chichester Pevensey

Crediton Wimborne Bosham
R. Vamar Exeter Dorchester
Wareham

CORNWALL Portland Corfe *Isle of Wight*
St Germans Dartmouth

ENGLISH CHANNEL

more modest expectations than the frenchified Normans of the Norman Conquest. They were men who expected to do their own farming, not to be lords of manors, and they greatly strengthened the large class who were later to be called yeomen, accepting an obligation to serve in arms when called upon and to meet certain other clearly-defined local obligations, but otherwise freemen. Below them, both in the Danelaw and in Wessex, there was a lower class who were not free to leave their agricultural employment on which the harvest, and so the life of the community, depended. In their document Alfred and Guthrum agreed on equal *wergilds*, or money payments, when a Dane or Saxon was killed, and a higher *wergild* in gold for men of higher rank, but always with the principle that, like for like, the Saxons and the Danes were equal.

Guthrum settled in East Anglia, and until his death in 890 could be relied on as a friendly neighbour. But Alfred's wars with the Danes were not over. Throughout the eighties the *Chronicle* records there was great Danish activity in the Carolingian Empire, culminating in the protracted siege of Paris in 888 and in the cession of Normandy to Roll, its first Duke, in 911. A name which occurred often in the mainland wars was that of the formidable Danish commander Haesten and in 892 he turned his attention to England, sailing at the head of a fleet of at least 250 ships from Boulogne to the Kent coast. There seems little doubt that these Danes came to England because the opposition of the Franks was proving too much for them. New Frankish commanders were emerging, among them the men who were to be the founders of the House of Capet, which was to rule France for the next nine hundred years. The inept descendants of Charlemagne had proved unequal to the challenger they had to meet, and at the end of the ninth century they disappear from the seats of even nominal power, accompanied by such jeering epithets as 'the Fat', 'the Bald' and 'the Simple', reflections on their personal characteristics, which indicate how they had lost all respect. The new leaders were much more local and limited in their ambitions, so that we are at the beginning of the local dynasties which were to be the pivots of the political history of Europe.

At first Alfred tried to negotiate with Haesten, along the lines which had answered with Guthrum. Haesten agreed that

Viking Art

Although the Scandanavian raiders were considered
destructive barbarians by the countries they invaded,
their art was highly developed and they brought
with them styles which were to have considerable
influence on Anglo-Saxon design.

RIGHT A carved head showing a nose-piece helmet.
BELOW One of the richly-carved sleighs found in the
Oseberg ship burial. It bears marks of wear but is too
elaborate to have been for every-day use.

OPPOSITE ABOVE The Sigurd Saga depicted on a
carved rock in Sweden shows a legendary hero
slaying a dragon and (far left) a decapitated smith
with his head and hammer falling through the air.

BELOW A Viking tombstone from St Paul's churchyard, tenth or eleventh century. The backward-looking head, spiral hips, claw-like feet and long curled tendrils are typical of the vivacious style known as Ringerike – a mingling of Viking and English art.

his two sons should be baptised, with Alfred standing as god-father to one and his son-in-law Ethelred of Mercia standing godfather to the other. But this did not prevent Haesten from establishing himself in Guthrum's old kingdom and, from the fortified strongpoint of Benfleet on the Essex coast, cutting off London with a fleet of Danish ships. Then the large body of Danes, which had been landed in Kent, tried to make their way north through the Weald, the *foresta* of the Andred's Weald, which has been described as though it were an impenetrable forest of trees, but which can hardly have been impenetrable, for it was, after all, the country through which Harold was to march from London to resist William the Conqueror. Although the *Anglo-Saxon Chronicle* has plenty to say about this, it remains obscure why this very ambitious enterprise fizzled out. There was no great battle, but the Danes seem to have lacked sufficient forces to advance westward, despite the support of the Danish King Guthfrith of York in Northumbria, who sent an expedition to Exeter (a town which seems to have had an irresistible attraction for the Danes, probably with the belief that as the Cornishmen were not Saxons, they would join forces with them). All that we know for certain is that Alfred was able to relieve Exeter without any great difficulty, and that in the final phase of the third and last of Alfred's wars, the Danes did not even recapture London; that Edward, Alfred's son and not unworthy successor, and Ethelred of Mercia organised a large force against them; that the River Lea was successfully obstructed by Alfred's forces so that the Danes could not use it to penetrate to London, and that their ships were useless to them, and those that were the wrong side of the blocking boom which the Saxons had interposed, had to be abandoned. The only engagement which can rank as a pitched battle was at Farnham, which was won by Edward and his Mercian brother-in-law, but Alfred was still very active, pursuing the Danes now to Exeter now to Bridgnorth in Mercia, with organised relays of troops.

In 896 the Danes began to disperse. Those who had marketable booty settled among their fellow-Danes as far as Northumbria, but the others, the moneyless ones, recrossed the Channel to try their fortunes once more in France, fortunes which were to improve to the point that fifteen years later, the

OPPOSITE The 'Beatus Page' from an Anglo-Saxon psalter of the early eleventh century.

Be
ATVS VIR QVI NON
ABIIT IN CONSILIO IMPIO
RVM

Two remnants of the
Danish occupation
of London.
RIGHT A ninth-century
sword pommel of carved
silver inlaid with niello,
found in Fetter Lane,
depicts a series of writhing
snakes. The pommel is
four inches long.
OPPOSITE A stirrup with
brass inlay found in the
Thames near the Tower.

Franks agreed to cede the rich lands which became Normandy,
the home of the Northmen. This last Danish campaign had
been a very ambitious one, and apparently concerted with the
Danes already settled in England, so that the years 892–4 produce a situation that for a time looked almost as menacing as the
critical year 878. But Alfred was in one key respect in a much
stronger strategic position. Through the peace with Guthrum,
Wessex had replaced Mercia in control of London, and if the
Danes had to stop short of the Medway and call for help from

Essex it was because they could not, as earlier fleets had done, penetrate beyond London. Furthermore, the Danes had on this occasion brought their wives and children with them, from which it is legitimate inference that the fighting men in the 250 vessels should not be taken as, at the most, forty to a ship, but something rather less.

One feature of Alfred's defensive policy which was not carried out as thoroughly as the King wished was the building of strongpoints, the *burhs*. A document survives from the early

tenth century, called the *'Burgalhidage'*, which lists the *burhs* and the lands for their support. Unfortunately the work was in many places neglected after some rudimentary beginning, and proved inadequate when put to the test. Asser writes of the bitter but vain remorse felt by these negligent officials and thanes when the heathen overran the inadequate defences, plundered them of their possessions and very often carried off their wives and children.

However, when we read how readily the *ealdormen* of Somerset and Wiltshire, no less than Hampshire and Berkshire, came into Hertfordshire, Surrey and Sussex, it is clear that the Saxon morale was high, and the story from the beginning very different to that in the late seventies. The credit for this plainly belongs to Alfred. It is highly significant that he was in relations not only with the Danes of East Anglia and north-east Mercia but with the Northumbrian Danes, and took oaths and hostages from them. That they abandoned the hostages and broke the oaths is less significant than that the Saxon kingdom of Wessex was in a position to make these demands, and we can already see in the last decade of Alfred's reign the foreshadowing of the next fifty years. Under Alfred's son Edward, who has never received his proper recognition as one of the builders of the English Crown, and under his three sons who reigned in turn, the Saxons prevailed over the Danes. Alfred's grandson Athelstan was the first King of the English to invade Scotland, a clear proof that his authority in Northumbria, though challenged constantly by the Danes who had their stronghold in Dublin and came across the sea to Lancashire, was real authority, sufficient both to hold a council in York and to endow the shrine of St Cuthbert at Durham. It was there that the monk Simeon of Durham wrote, a hundred years after Alfred's death, one of the fullest accounts of his reign. If perhaps there is some imagination, there is also throughout a sense that in commemorating Alfred, he is not commemorating a foreign prince. Thus he attributes the decisive victory of Ethandune to Alfred's devotion to St Cuthbert, and to St Cuthbert's powerful aid, where Asser attributes it to Alfred's southern kinsman St Neot, who, he tells us, appeared to the King the night before the battle, and bade him have no fear, for all would be well, St Neot would be with him and would go before him.

OPPOSITE The head of Alfred from a coin of the reign shows him clean-shaven with a determined chin.

Splendid examples of
Scandinavian carving.
RIGHT AND OPPOSITE
Two carved head-posts
from the Oseberg ship
burial, probably
ornaments on vehicles
used for religious
ceremonial. Such heads are
commonly carved with
open jaws or teeth bared
ready for attack.
CENTRE LEFT The wooden
prow of an eighth-century
Viking ship dredged from
the River Scheldt, Belgium.
CENTRE RIGHT The flat
head of a bed-post from
the Gokstad find.

TOP A penny struck *c.* 880 with the obverse
inscription AELFRED REX ANGLOR (UM) –
Alfred, King of the English – shows that by this date
Alfred was ranked as more than King of Wessex.
The reverse is copied from that of a late Roman coin.
ABOVE A fine penny struck after Alfred's
occupation of London in 886 with a monogram
of LONDONIA on the reverse side.

When at long last Alfred's line ceased to produce brave and competent young kings, and his great-great-grandson Ethelred, who lives in history as 'the Unready' or foolish king, lost so much of the ground gained, there was one vital difference. Between him and his Danish adversaries the prize was what it was to be for the next five hundred years, a single crown. Whoever prevailed would be king of the whole island, and it was in that spirit that Ethelred was succeeded by King Canute. He reigned over Danes and Saxons impartially, and could even be succeeded by his two short-lived and inadequate sons, and then the same single crown could with general consent be brought back into Alfred's line with Edward the Confessor.

3
The Ruler
of the
Kingdom

For THE ANGLO-SAXONS, as for other Germanic peoples, law rested on custom, on agreed and immemorial usage, and a ruler, when he acted as a law-giver, saw himself as setting out what the law was, not as creating it. If he made innovations to meet new problems or conditions, he did so cautiously, with the advice of his wise men. The first Anglo-Saxon laws that have come down to us in written form are those of Ethelbert, the King of Kent, who received and was converted by the monks sent from Rome by Pope Gregory. That Pope had himself spent ten years in Constantinople, only a few years after the death of the Emperor Justinian, the great codifier of Roman Civil Law, and we know from St Gregory's own writings, as well as from the inherent probability, that no one could live in Constantinople in a responsible position representing the Bishop of Rome without close acquaintance with Justinian's work. In accepting baptism for himself, with most of his people following his example, Ethelbert signified that he was also eager to accept a good deal more from Rome, and that a codification of the laws seemed to him a further step in civilisation. It was also necessary to incorporate into customary law new provisions arising out of the acceptance of the Catholic religion, for the Catholic Church itself had its own already elaborate juridical system after over two hundred years as the established religion of the Roman Empire. When the Church received lands and endowments, immunities and privileges from Ethelbert, it became highly advisable to make a record of them lest there should be conflict of testimony.

From Kent the idea of a written code was taken up in the seventh century in Wessex by King Ine, and in the eighth century in Mercia by Offa. When Alfred found himself king in a Wessex which included Kent and was beginning to include much which had been Mercia a century before, including the Severn Valley and London, he judged it useful to collect the laws of Ethelbert, Ine and Offa, and to harmonise them. His laws are avowedly a collection of pre-existent laws, and he puts forward his own suggestions rather in the spirit of a Government White Paper for discussion than as a Bill for enactment. He was also much exercised that although his people had been Christians for over two centuries, much of their law had originated in their pre-Christian past, and he wrote a long preface,

PREVIOUS PAGES A king in his court from a tenth-century manuscript.

104

looking all the time to the Bible, and in particular to the Old Testament, whose law Christ had come not to destroy but to fulfill, so that it had not lost all its relevance to the followers of Christ, although they were Gentiles not Jews.

A silver penny of King Offa of Mercia, who dominated England in the eighth century and whose code of laws was included in Alfred's collection.

A century before Alfred's time, the rite of coronation had been introduced among the Germans by St Boniface. He drew heavily on the Old Testament narrative of the prophet Samuel crowning Saul, to make kingship a sacred office, in a sustained attempt to help the rulers of the Dark Ages curb the temptations to which their power exposed them. The coronation was the occasion of taking a solemn oath, and the stone is still to be seen at Kingston-upon-Thames in Surrey where the kings of the Wessex dynasty were crowned in turn, from Egbert to his grandsons' grandsons, with the exception of one of them, Edgar, who was crowned at Bath. As the king took the oath, so through the lesser ranks of society the oath and the pledge were the cement which kept the social fabric together.

Alfred's laws are in general humane, resting firmly on the principle that a man's life could be atoned for by a payment to his relatives, the *wergild*, which varied according to a man's rank, and just as a life could be paid for, so also could a limb or an eye. We get a vivid impression of the violence of the time, the continuance of family feuds. If a man was called on to follow his lord to war, he would have to rely on a neighbour to look

after his livestock; when he returned he might find the livestock no longer there, and be told by the neighbour that marauders had stolen them; he might have a strong suspicion that nothing of the sort had happened, and that his neighbour had sold the livestock. If he believed this, he could call on the neighbour to purge himself with a solemn oath, but he must not take the law into his own hands. Alfred, in his preface to his collection of laws, or 'dooms', plainly has chiefly in mind those who have to give judgment in such cases, and who will be under constant temptation to favour one or other party, not according to the merits of the case but for fear or favour. Thus Alfred invokes the golden rule that no man should give a judgment which he would be unwilling to see given against himself. The great protection of private property in Anglo-Saxon society was the difficulty of disposing of it without the transactions becoming known, and the beginnings of the jury system rested on the principle that one of the best guides to who was telling the truth was the good name or the less good name that a man enjoyed among his neighbours. The guiding principle was exactly the opposite of what was later to become the essence of the jury system, that the jurors must have no previous knowledge of the parties to a suit and if possible no knowledge of the facts or preconceived opinions. The jury system was not developed in Alfred's time, but in the local court, the proceedings were in public, and a local public opinion was presumably often the chief guide for the thane or reeve whose court it was and whose business it was to give judgment.

Judgment by Ordeal was a widespread custom among the peoples of northern Europe, in this very much behind the Roman Empire. When the Germanic tribes became Christians instead of having recourse to Wodin, they moved the Ordeal into a Christian setting, leaving its organisation to the local clergy. The governing idea was an appeal to God to give a sign to show where the truth lay when there was a direct conflict of testimony, or when purely circumstantial evidence was repudiated by the accused on oath. Those who were called on to face the Ordeal were taken in hand by the clergy; they fasted for three days, made their confession and were solemnly adjured not to tempt retribution by proclaiming their innocence if they were not innocent. There were then four kinds of Ordeal which took place in the presence of the plaintiff in a civil action, with twelve supporters to see that there was no tampering with the test. The simplest and most painless Ordeal was to eat a specially baked cake with the invitation that it might choke the accused if he was lying, and this was the famous end of the great Earl Godwin in Guildford Castle, when he swore he had no hand in the sudden death of Edward the Confessor's elder brother Alfred, but choked and died. Much more painful was the Ordeal by cold water in which the accused was bound hand and foot and put in a deep pool, but with a rope attached. If he was innocent he was supposed to sink and could then be pulled up before he died by drowning, but if he should float he was adjudged guilty. This form of Ordeal far outlasted all the other forms, and was used against women charged with witchcraft as late as the seventeenth century.

Even more alarming were the Ordeals by fire. In one, the accused had to plunge his bare arm into boiling water and fetch out a stone from the bottom of the vessel. His arm was then bandaged and left for three days. At the end of the time, priests, in the presence of witnesses, unbandaged the arm which had to be wholly healed for him to be acquitted. The other Ordeal by

Ploughing in January. This scene and those following are from the monthly pictures of a Saxon calendar, one of the few surviving documents which illustrate the daily life of the people.

fire was even more drastic, and consisted of carrying a very hot iron rod for a number of paces, and there again the test of innocence was that if there were any burns they should all disappear in three days. The last form of Ordeal, the duel, came in after the Anglo-Saxon period, continued to the very end of the Middle Ages and was the parent of the duel fought not to seek a judgment from Heaven but in defence of a man's honour, which lasted well into the nineteenth century in Britain, and even later on the Continent. Pope Stephen v attacked Judgment by Ordeal as superstitious as early as 816, but papal prohibitions and condemnations had to be reiterated over four centuries before the practice finally disappeared at the end of the twelfth century in England in the legal reforms of Henry II.

Only in a few instances was the death penalty exacted. Those who engaged in sorcery or 'commerce with devils' were not to be suffered to live, and for nearly a thousand years this was to be a constant hazard facing eccentric old women living by themselves and inspiring awe and revulsion in the village, unless they had stout-hearted kinsfolk to vouch for them and stand by them. When Alfred is making an exception to the general rule that most penalties can be reduced to money terms, the

TROPIC CAPRICORNES
·1·LUNA·
UM ĝēſ conciditur agnuſ·
nordine quadriſ·
ſanguine fulget·
gauiſque kalendaſ·
rum iueſtice uater·

February: cutting wood.

March: digging
and sowing.

MENSEHUME RE IHMED

C M

.XI H E 1111 Ñ Erquadris

.XIX E E O E 111 Ñ Trinisiam

VIII P G 11 Ñ Pridie par

PROCEDUNT SUPPLI ΤΕΣ INM

MAE HIDIIS

III A A D MARI· EGIE

D B E VI Ñ Sexas mnon

XI C F V Ñ viriferunt

F B E D G 1111 Ñ Octeria qua

XIX F A 111 Ñ Septimuf

CONSTAT SIDERE AQUARI ÷

...ES LUNA XXIX·

...um brigida soraca ktas.
...plo deducitur archis.
...renaus emine altas.
...rtus & nomine magnus.

3

...EPORE PISCES.
...LUNA XXX
...AGIUS MARTIS QUERITQUE kt'
...uerat accula paulus.
...npus procedit abantris.
...no milite fulgent.
...f procedit tempore turno.

outstanding exception is that if a man is untrue to his lord and plots against him to the peril of the lord's life, then the offender must pay the penalty with his own life. The right of sanctuary is recognised, especially in what we may call approved monasteries, to which the king gave money to enable the monks to feed the hungry and serve their neighbour in the other corporal works of mercy. Sanctuary, the principle that no one could be arrested in a church, had its time-limit which was generally seven days, and in some cases the church authorities had to provide food, in others a man's kinsfolk were to bring it to him. Glimpses of a high civilisation appear in a provision of penalties for 'the stealer of gold', 'the stealer of stud horses, the stealer of bees'; the fines, Alfred tells us, used to vary but had now been made uniform, the only exception with a heavier fine was for those who stole a man, and it is not quite clear what this meant. Men were stolen sometimes by marauding bandits to be carried into captivity, but the word 'kidnap' does not enter the English language until the end of the seventeenth century in connection with the American plantations to which young children might be seized and shipped for the value of their labour.

There are fines for lesser forms of theft, like the felling of another man's trees, five shillings for a large tree but only fivepence for the succeeding trees; if a man should accidentally

kill another, as by letting the tree he was felling fall on the other man, the tree was to be given to the kinsmen, presumably in addition to the *wergild*. Then there are provisions against baby-farming if the children should die while being fostered; and there are compensations fixed for the contingency of a be-trothed maiden committing fornication – if she is of churlish birth, sixty shillings compensation to be paid in cattle and not to include any slave. This is one of the few references to the existence of this lowest class in the community, although by the constant reference to free men it is abundantly clear that there was a large class who were not free, although some of them lived in a state of partial bondage, being tied to the soil in order to ensure that the work of the farm would be done, but not liable to be sold away from it. And there is a very curious provision which lays down that if anyone entrusts property to 'another man's monk' without the permission of the monk's lord, and the monk then loses it, the original owner must bear its loss and not have any claim against the monk's lord, presumably his religious superior. But perhaps the origin of the idea that every dog, in addition to having his day, is entitled to one bite, comes from these laws of Alfred; the dogs and their owners get off very lightly. We read that if a dog rends or tears a man to death, it will cost the dog's owner six shillings for the first offence, and

May: watching sheep.

TAURI·

UNA XX.

OBUS MERUIT PHILIPPUSQ: MICAAE KLDIS.

RIA COGNOMINE SENIS·

ET INUENTIO LIGNI·

uni dequacol

E   o

R
DIES·X

LIVNI·

XIX   I   P   F   IIII   N   inquadrif c
VIII   C   Q   G   III   N   coeabuf ar
XVI   I   k   R   A   II   N   Ante diem

July: haymaking.

if he feeds the dog after its misdeed and the dog then rends a
second man, the owner is to pay twelve shillings, and for a
third rending, thirty shillings. This suggests that the dogs of
Anglo-Saxon England were massive beasts, kept for the hunt
and a vigorous outdoor life, and it was a favourite present for
Alfred himself to give wolf-hounds.

Then there is a quite sudden outburst of ferocity against
slander, for the penalty for public slander is to be no lighter
penalty than cutting off the slanderer's tongue, though here the
tongue can be saved by a payment of a proportion of the *wergild*
at which the man's whole life is valued. It is rather odd to find
that, while scourging a churl leads to a penalty of twenty shillings,
the much more serious injury of blinding him costs only six
shillings, while if he is put in the stocks that is considered so
much more serious, five times as serious as being blinded, that

the compensation is to be thirty shillings. If, as an insult, he cuts the churl's hair, that is thought serious enough to warrant a ten shilling fine, whereas if he tonsures him like a priest, that costs thirty shillings, ten shillings more than the fine for cutting off his beard. The accidental dangers of going about one's business, the Anglo-Saxon equivalent of the danger we face in a motor-car, included the risk of being transfixed accidentally by another man's spear, and there are fines for this which are measured by the angle at which the spear was held, that angle being thought relevant to any charge of intent. The royal dignity is constantly protected, for the fines are much more severe if at a public meeting a weapon is drawn in the presence of the king's representative, the *earldorman* or a reeve.

After we have grown used all the time to ten, twenty or thirty shillings as the fine for these personal injuries, it is rather

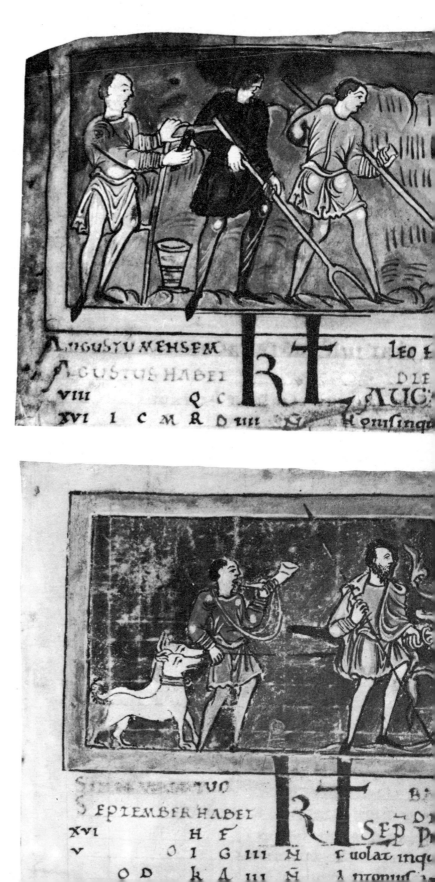

AUGUSTU MEHSEM
GUSTUS HABEI   LEO ɛ
VIII   Q C   DLE
XVI I C M R D III N AUG

SEPTEMBER HABEI
XVI   H F   SEP
V   O I G III N f uolat inqu
O D K A III N A

S IGNE P URIT.

LUNA. XXIX:.

MERITO TRADUNTUR SEPE KALENDE.

ephanus preuiderat alta.

August: scything.

September: hunting and
pasturing swine.

EPTEMBER QUINAF.

X. LUNA. XXX.

T PRIMAS UIRGO SCAQUE KALENDAS.

goniuf omne nonif.

ta. fcandere minif.

surprising to read how heavy and severe is the penalty for breaking the Church's rules about the Lenten fast without securing permission; that the compensation to be paid is 120 shillings. Compensation is surely the wrong word, for who has been injured when a man has not kept the Lenten fast? In general, the disappearance in later law of the principle of compensation to the victim or injured party, in addition to the fine payable to the Crown, is something we must regret. It is elementary justice, but it is only in the twentieth century that penal reformers have become seriously concerned to reintroduce it, and to devise ways by which men in prison can earn more and so make a real contribution, not only to the cost of the prison, but to reimbursing the victim and putting by something which will help them to go straight on their release. In Anglo-Saxon law we find very little about imprisonment, and the fortified *burhs* which Alfred constructed were primarily earthworks with wooden buildings from which it would not have been easy to prevent escapes. Even when the epoch of castles built of stone came in with the Normans, we constantly read of escapes, and as constantly of the foulness of the dungeons which were the most secure as well as the most unpleasant features of these castles.

November: fencing and keeping warm.

S cos etus liberatiu   T præceps
HOUEMBER HABET   D1 ES : X
     O D C K D   HOUE (
   XIII   L   E IIII N H omis inqu
   II   D M F III N G ermanus

One curious provision, quite unnecessary in the codes of the earlier lawgivers collected by Alfred, is against half-freemen or slaves defecting and joining the Danish army. Though it is said that they must not go without permission, it is difficult to imagine permission being given, and it is laid down that defecting Danes are not to be received into the Saxon *fyrd*. Trade with the Danes might be permitted for mutual advantage, but such exchanges of cattle or goods are to be accompanied by an exchange of hostages as proof of good faith. These provisions do not come from the laws but from the treaty between Alfred and Guthrum made a good many years after Guthrum's baptism in 878, and dated 886.

Provision for holidays is also made in the laws of Alfred. They are holidays only for freemen, not for slaves or unfree labourers, but for their beneficiaries they were more generous than the Englishmen of the eighteenth or nineteenth century could imagine. At the turn of the year, there were twelve days at Christmas. Then came a feast which has somehow slipped from the Church's calendar, the day that Christ overcame the Devil, presumably the temptations in the desert, which was commemorated on 25 February. Then, in gratitude, there came 12 March, the feast of the Apostle of the English, Pope St Gregory

Tɛɾɱɪɲat àɾɪ αɲɪɲſ
ꝯ CIBER HABET
XIIII Q D D � ɛ
II   A G IIII H   Z tꝗ: ſecꝰ

the Great, with seven days at Easter for Holy Week and seven
days after Easter for rejoicing. The feast of St Peter and St Paul
followed on 29 June, the feast of the Assumption on 15 August
and finally the Feast of All Saints, 1 November. The slaves
were given the four Wednesdays in the four Ember Weeks on
which they could sell anything they had been given in Christian
charity or the produce of their leisure moments. The curious
omissions in this list are Ascension Day and the great feast of
Whitsun ten days later. Those came with the Norman kings.

It is a sad commentary on the reality of the Norman Conquest
that the words 'churl' and 'churlish', 'villain' and 'villainous',
have such very bad connotations, for they were simply the
names of the lesser orders of English society over which the
Norman invaders had come to rule. In Alfred's day *ceorls*
were men who later were to be called the yeomen of England,
peasant small-holders. Their *wergild* was a sixth of a thane's,

ıa fıeı ơ ơecembri
xxı·Luni · x · x·
es mensis kisiahum continet dixum.
auctorem possidet dequum·
cum magno nomine scm.

December: winnowing.

twelve hundred shillings, and two hundred shillings or one
thousand silver pennies was no mean capital sum. The *ceorls*
provided the basis of the *fyrd* who were supposed to follow the
ealdorman of the shire, or perhaps their local thane, to the king's
wars. A *ceorl* was quite likely to own a slave, but we are left with
very little information beyond the knowledge that there was an
unfree class. In a famous passage, Alfred says that a king needs
three classes of subjects, his men for prayer, churchmen; his
men for war, the *fyrd* men; and his men for work; from this
some historians have argued that there was no universal military
obligation, that some of the king's subjects were exempted
from answering the call to arms because the essential business of
agriculture had to be carried on. What is disputed is whether
this was done on a basis of individual exemption, as in the wars
of the twentieth century, when certain men were exempted
or refused permission to enlist because they were engaged on

The splendid Anglo-Saxon objects discovered at
Sutton Hoo (see p. 130) were obviously such as only
royal houses would possess. The craftsmanship of
more common goods is illustrated here.

BELOW Ornaments from a woman's grave, *c*. 600,
at Wheatley near Oxford: a pair of brooches worn
as fasteners of dresses at the shoulder; a string of
beads, probably slung between the brooches rather
than around the neck, which are mostly of amber but
include some opaque coloured glass; a corroded iron
buckle; a bronze pin with a gilded head and a
silver ring.

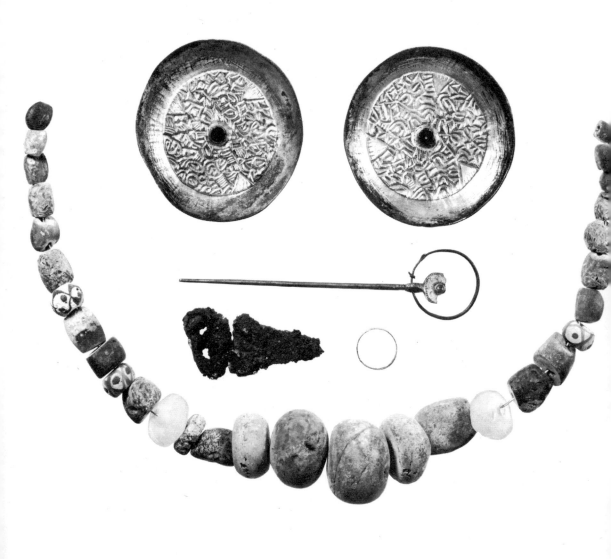

LEFT A cooking pot.
BELOW Keys and key-ring found at Reculver.

work of national importance, or whether there were classes like the unfree who were excluded from the right and duty of bearing arms; this latter seems probable enough where there would have been the greater temptation to desert and to join the enemy, if that was the only way of obtaining the status of a free man.

It is curious that the word 'thane', which meant so much in Anglo-Saxon England, entirely disappeared from social usage in the Middle Ages. Most existing titles, dukes, marquesses, earls, viscounts, all go back directly to military commands and territorial responsibilities, reflecting the structure of medieval society. There were no dukes before the Norman Conquest, and it was the Danes who brought in the title of *jarl* or earl, and count and viscount are also post-Conquest. The thane was supplanted after the Norman Conquest by two titles which have endured to this day, baron and knight, but essentially the function was the same for them all, that they were fighting men who held large estates and in return came themselves and brought their dependants to the field to serve in war under the king and his *ealdormen* of the shires. Alfred would not have known the words 'knight' which was to come from Germany or 'baron' which was to come from France, but he knew very well the essential role in society which had to be fulfilled by the large local landowners. They not only had paramount duty in war, but had also to play a part in the administering of justice, especially in the settling of disputes between neighbours. The rewards for administering justice and exacting fines were always eyed covetously by the kings, and little by little the royal justice became more and more important, and was one of the main achievements of the Norman dynasty. Alfred had to rely on his *ealdormen* and his thanes, reserving an ultimate power of adjudication to himself, but on no very clear principle. It would depend on where the king was and how he regarded the subject matter in dispute. When Asser came to his Court in the middle eighties, Alfred was already a king with authority, only in his thirties but with a great record of achievement behind him. Asser tells us how he supervised his *ealdormen* and thanes in their administration of justice. He looked closely into their decisions to discover whether they had been acting from partiality or any unworthy motive, or had made what he judged a bad decision from ignorance. In that case they were told that they must either acquit themselves better and give their minds to the law, or else give up their offices.

There are many indications of Alfred's continually growing prestige. Asser himself found that his fellow-monks at St David's agreed to his going to reside at Alfred's Court because they thought that even as far away from south-western Wales so powerful a king would help them with their local ruler, who would hesitate before incurring the displeasure of the King of Wessex whose influence extended to south-west Mercia and the lower Severn Valley. Alfred's grandfather, Egbert, had made expeditions which, according to the *Anglo-Saxon Chronicle*, had quickly reduced the various Welsh kings to humble submission. But these Welsh kings maintained a relative independence against their powerful neighbour the King of England down to the early fifteenth century, and their country was not formally incorporated into the English state until the time of Henry VIII.

They have indeed the distinction of being politically among the last survivors of Roman imperial government, which operated through local rulers or sub-kings, like Herod in Judea, and the kings – King Lear was one of them – who ruled in Roman Britain and who are recorded by Geoffrey of Monmouth, as he claimed, from written as well as from oral tradition. It is possible that Alfred had some vague suzerainty acknowledged by the Northumbrians. The princes of Northumbria had given such a vague recognition to Charlemagne, perhaps through the influence of Alcuin of York, their countryman, and in the hope that the patronage of so great a ruler might bring them assistance when they found themselves the first victims of ferocious Danish onslaughts at the end of the eighth century. Chroniclers not very far removed in time from Alfred's reign tell the story of how the Abbot of Wearmouth had a vision of St Cuthbert who told him to go and find a boy of ten, Guthred by name, who had to be ransomed from captivity, but who was predestined to be accepted by the Danes as their king in Northumbria. We do not know how he achieved the throne, and it is not certain that he is the same as Cnut, but it is probable from the dates that the Danish name might have been adopted to satisfy his Danish subjects. The point of his story is that a silver penny has been found with his

Christianity was the chief inspiration of the subject-matter of art all over the British Isles, although pagan traditions frequently survived in the design.

RIGHT The loaves and fishes and the flight into Egypt depicted on the base of the Moone Cross, Eire. BELOW A pair of silver christening spoons bearing the names of Saul and Paul in Greek, from Sutton Hoo.

An Anglo-Saxon cross, known as the Rupert Cross, from the eighth or ninth century. The twisted tendrils are reminders of pre-Christian art.

A bronze image of Thor
the Thunderer, the noblest
and most powerful of
Norse gods, clasping his
hammer; the figure was
found in Iceland.

name on one side and that of Alfred on the other, as though Cnut was willing to see himself as ruling in one part of the island of which Alfred was the chief ruler. Simeon of Durham says that when Guthred or Cnut died in 894 it rested with Alfred to decide who should be the next ruler of Northumbria.

The effect of the Danish invasions, beginning as they did with the pillaging, murdering and burning in Christian monasteries and churches, made all the tribes who formed the nation of the English extremely conscious that, however much they might have fought with each other, they were all bound together by the same fate and living inside the Church which was organised on a national basis. When Offa was far the most important of the English kings, he resented that the chief archbishoprics were not in Mercia but in Kent and Northumbria, and he tried unsuccessfully to obtain the Pope's sanction for a new archbishopric at Lichfield and the transfer of the southern archbishopric to London. The juridical nature of the Catholic Church helped Angles and Saxons and Jutes to feel themselves to be first and foremost Christians, and it was in terms of Christians *versus* Pagans that the wars with the Danes are described. Hence it came about that Alfred, as a victor in that struggle, even though he had had to concede to the Danes an extensive right of settlement, was looked on by the Christians everywhere as their leader. Asser uses this title of him, 'Leader of the Christians', in front of his kingly title, in the fragment of his Life which was presented to Bishop Werferth of Worcester as one of the King's most valued collaborators in his literary enterprises.

This title of 'Leader of the Christians' was historically important. Even before the Danish invasion, the monk-chronicler Bede had recognised an underlying unity so that Anglo-Saxons and Jutes could all be called the English nation, at least by a historian primarily interested in them as Christians and calling his work *Ecclesiastical History*. Equally, there was a common Christianity shared with inhabitants of the island who were not Angles or Saxons or Jutes, and undoubtedly the violence of the Danes played its part in bringing out even between Celt and Saxon what they had in common as Christians. The Welsh chieftains, Celtic by blood, came to have a respect for Alfred, whose influence was so strong in the Severn Valley.

The Sutton Hoo Treasure

In 1939 excavation at Sutton Hoo, on the River Deben in south-east Suffolk, revealed a buried ship loaded with treasure but containing no body, believed to be a cenotaph to an East Anglian king. The hoard of gold coins indicated that the burial took place in the mid-seventh century. The treasure included some magnificent examples of Anglo-Saxon workmanship.

RIGHT Gold clasps inset with garnets and glass.
ABOVE A gold purse with the frame and plaques of inlaid garnet and mosaic glass.
LEFT A gold buckle with interlace ornament.

It must also always be borne in mind that 'Christians' meant for those who used the term in Alfred's day, members of the highly organised and juridical Catholic Church under the Pope in Rome. To be a Christian was to become a member of a society with a great many rules and regulations, and penalties for failing to observe them, and this common membership of an organised society was a bond between men of varying races long before the Jutes, Saxons and Angles were converted by Pope Gregory's mission and by the other missionaries authorised from Rome on condition that they worked in new mission fields. For there is much evidence that Catholic Christianity had been implanted among the Romano-British population. A sub-king under the Romans, Lucius by name, had made the journey to Rome to be baptised by Pope Eleutherius (174–189). Roman soldiers stationed in Britain, who brought in other creeds like that of Mithras, whose temple has been found in London, were some of them Christians. The Roman legionaries did not depart until 410, almost exactly a century after the Edict of Milan had given full toleration to the Christians, and Constantine, first proclaimed as Emperor in York, had made the fourth century the beginnings of Christendom with the official conversion of the Roman Empire. St Augustine and his companions found a church in Canterbury dedicated to St Martin, who did not die until 400, and Ethelbert, their host, had a Frankish Catholic wife for whom, indeed, the church may have been provided.

The proto-martyr of Britain, St Alban, was a victim of the last great persecution, and died in 303. In 314 we find three British bishops, one of them Bishop of London, taking part in the Council of Arles. Yet it was not a British but a Saxon hostelry that was established in Rome to meet the needs of the steady stream of pilgrims from the island, and that is evidence that the Saxons threw themselves much more whole-heartedly into their conversion than the Romano-British had done. It may well be that they had a greater devotion to Rome, the Papacy and the tombs of the Apostles, because it had all come to them as something new and wonderful, while those who had lived in Britain as a province of the Roman empire had never felt the same awe and reverence.

But it must not be thought that the Catholic Church had

A bronze censer-cover from Canterbury in the form of a building, tenth to eleventh century. The lower borders and hips of the animals are inlaid with nielloed silver plates.

everything its own way. In Alfred's last decade, Pope Formosus (891–6) wrote a very stiff letter to the Archbishop of Canterbury, saying that he had heard 'that the abominable rites of the pagans had revived in your country, and that like dumb dogs you kept silent. We were minded to cut you off from the body of the Church.' It could be, of course, that it was not only among the Danes that pagan practices revived, and the term 'pagan practice' is a wide one. Indeed, some country customs of the present time can be traced back to pagan times, and throughout the Middle Ages the Church authorities were engaged in a constant battle with superstitious practices which persisted. However, the Archbishop thus threatened, though it does not seem to have been any more than a threat, was the last man to deserve it. Plegmund by name, he first emerges into history as a hermit in retreat near Chester on land which, surprisingly belonged to King Ethelwulf of Wessex. We know that Ethelwulf in his will shows that he owned land on his own account, apart from that which belonged to him as King of Wessex. This was presumably such an estate, and because of the royal connection, Alfred came to know of the hermit, his holiness and learning, and induced him to leave his chosen way of life and come to the royal Court to help the King with his translations and studies. He made so good an impression that when the see of Canterbury fell vacant, Alfred nominated him for it.

Plegmund reigned in the see of Canterbury until 911, during which time the Papacy had a succession of unworthy popes, and Formosus himself is chiefly remembered for the gross indignities to which he was exposed after his death. His successor, Stephen vi, had the body of Formosus exhumed, and staged a macabre trial in which, as the dead man refused to plead, he was adjudged guilty, and his corpse thrown into the Tiber; the charges against him being that he had tolerated dishonesty and licentiousness. The real truth was that the great lay nobles, the Houses of Tusculum and Spoleto, taking advantage of the custom that the laity as well as the clergy should elect the Bishop of Rome in spite of the world-wide character which his office had acquired and held for over four centuries, not only produced their own candidates, but vilified those of the opposite faction. The immediate successor of Formosus only lived for a fortnight after his election, and thereupon the Spoletan faction put in Stephen vi, who disgraced himself and the papacy by holding the trial of Formosus. There was one far-reaching practical consequence; Formosus was declared not to have been canonically elected, although it was not denied that he had been bishop of a small place called Portus. It was laid down that all the clergy whom he had ordained as Pope must be reordained. From that it seemed to follow that all the acts of his pontificate

134

were invalid throughout the Universal Church and must be re-confirmed, often with appropriate penance. Pope Stephen himself soon met with retribution. He was seized by his enemies, thrown into prison and strangled.

A new synod repudiated the grisly synod which had condemned Formosus after his death, and laid down that for the future, the trial of corpses was forbidden, and all who had taken part in it had to beg for mercy from the new Pope, John IX. In all this unedifying episode in Rome, the representative of Arnulf, the German emperor, played a part. His name was Lambert, and he seems to have been equally unfavourably impressed by the Tusculum and Spoletan factions, and there is presaged the more decisive German interventions of the tenth century. The distance of Wessex from Rome had its compensations. We do not know how much was known to Alfred or how he took the reports which, presumably, came from the turbulent city. But when Alfred died, his son and successor received a sharp and indignant letter from Pope John IX, saying that he had heard that many sees were vacant in England, and that elections were to be made at once under pain of excommunication. The authority of Rome was such that the King of Wessex hastily increased his bishops from two to five. Although the word *Curia* for the papal administration does not occur for another two hundred years, it is clear that there was an administrative machine that was functioning, keeping up a correspondence with archbishops and rulers in the name of the Popes, who were succeeding each other so rapidly, and often so violently, in an age when in the Church, as in the slowly-forming states, everything depended on the character, abilities and long continuance in office of the man at the top.

4
Religion and Learning

THE KING WHO HAS SUCH A CLAIM to have been the father of the Royal Navy has an equally strong claim to be called the father of English prose. Once the kingdom had been saved from the Danes, Alfred set himself to the restoration of religion and learning. There has survived a letter on that theme written by Alfred to one of his collaborators, Werferth, Bishop of Worcester in that part of Mercia which after Guthrum's conversion was left within the orbit of Wessex. It runs as follows:

Alfred King commandeth to great Werferth, bishop, with his words in loving and friendly wise: and I would have you informed that it has often come into my remembrance what wise men there formerly were among the English race, both of the sacred orders and the secular; and what happy times those were throughout the English race, and how the kings who had the government of the folk in those days obeyed God and His ministers; and they on the one hand maintained their peace and morality and their authority within their borders, while at the same time they enlarged their territory abroad; and how they prospered both in war and in wisdom; and also the sacred orders, how zealous they were both in teaching and in learning and in all the services which they owed to God: and how foreigners came to this land for wisdom and instruction; and how we should now have to get them from abroad if we were to have them. So clean was it fallen away in the English race that there were very few on this side Humber who could understand their mass-books in English, or translate a letter from Latin into English; and I ween that there were not many beyond the Humber. So few of them were there that I cannot think of so much as a single one south of the Thames when I came to the throne. ...

When I consider all this I remembered also how I saw, before it had all been ravaged and burnt, how the churches throughout England stood filled with treasures and books, and there was also a great multitude of God's servants, but they had very little knowledge of the books, for they could not understand anything of them because they were not written in their language. As if they had said: 'Our forefathers, who formerly held these places, loved wisdom, and through it they obtained wealth and bequeathed it to us. In this we can still see their tracks, but we cannot follow them, and therefore we have lost both the wealth and the wisdom, because we would not incline our hearts after their example.'

The scarcity of books and teachers was related to a decline in monastic life. When all books had to be copied by hand, in the Hellenistic world there had always been plenty of slaves sufficiently educated to act as copyists as well as to take down dictation, and very often the man dictating would be dictating to two secretaries at the same time, because of the much slower pace of handwriting compared with human speech. Before the age of shorthand, a man like Napoleon would habitually work by giving alternate sentences to two secretaries. The immensely copious writings of the Fathers of the Church must be seen in this light, with monks, probably the junior monks, as a great source for copyists, and the works of Alfred were sent to different monasteries or churches for such copies to be made.

The trouble was that in his day the monastic life was not flourishing. We have abundant evidence of this in the many letters which are extant from the Englishman Alcuin of York, at the beginning of the ninth century. Alcuin had been collected by Charlemagne just as Alfred, a hundred years later, collected men of learning wherever he could find them. Charlemagne had found them in Northumbria where he was just in time before the decline set in. The golden age of learning and the religious life in Northumbria lasted for just over a century, a century in which the whole life of the Venerable Bede was passed as a monk at Wearmouth. His contemporary St Egbert had founded the library at York, and St Benedict Biscop had been an abbot equally zealous for learning. But by the time Alfred was middle-aged, he was all too conscious that there had been a general decline, which would probably have occurred even without the appalling destruction by the Danes. If we take the conversion of the English as roughly completed around 650, the golden period which then set in lasted until just after the death of Bede in 735 and the birth of Alcuin about ten years later. But Alcuin, who had himself to be summoned to the great imperial Court at Aachen because of the lack of learned men in Charlemagne's wide dominions, was very conscious that both in his native Northumbria and in the rest of England, monastic life was losing its pristine fervour, and with it the scholarship which Bede had embodied. In the light of the general history of religious orders, the story is almost invariably the same, that the first fervour cannot be maintained, that little by little the rule is relaxed, particularly where there are large endowments; that

An enlargement of a section of the *Book of Kells*. In a small space at the foot of the initial is a miniature of two rats gnawing a church wafer, watched by two cats, carefully distinguished by the artist as a tortoise-shell and a brindled. Two more rats perch on their backs. It may be symbolic of the biblical prophesy that the lion and the lamb shall lie down together.

OPPOSITE The Crucifixion carved on an ivory plaque of tenth-century Anglo-Saxon workmanship.

BELOW LEFT The Pectoral Cross of St Cuthbert, found in the tomb of St Cuthbert in Durham Cathedral. It was presumably placed there on the saint's death in 687. Made of gold, shell and garnet, the cross is one of the latest pieces of garnet work in Anglo-Saxon jewellery. The cross is $2\frac{1}{2}$ inches wide.

LEFT Two portions of the stole of St Cuthbert, probably made at Winchester between 909 and 916, and presented to the shrine of St Cuthbert by King Athelstan.

OPPOSITE King Alfred's own introduction to his translation of Pope Gregory's *Pastoral Care*. It acted as a preface to all the works translated under his supervision, explaining his concern at the decay of learning in England and emphasising the need to revive it. He writes here how tragic it is that his people must go abroad to seek learning.

first the abbot begins to live well, then he has not the face to be too strict with his monks who know perfectly well how he is living, even when, as commonly happened in the Middle Ages, he had his own quarters and a country-house some distance from the abbey. As Alcuin's letters show, there was also much to be desired in the life of the secular clergy.

So it was altogether fitting that the first book Alfred put into Anglo-Saxon was one written by the Apostle of England, St Gregory's *Pastoral Care*. The English remained profoundly grateful to Pope Gregory. If, when they went to Rome, they were primarily seeking the tombs of St Peter and St Paul, they were also very conscious of St Gregory, and Alfred, who in other translations took considerable liberties with omissions and interpolations intended to make the work more palatable, was singularly scrupulous to translate *Pastoral Care* as literally as possible, as though it had almost the rank of Holy Scripture. Another of Pope Gregory's books, the *Dialogues*, was translated by Werferth, Bishop of Worcester, to whom the letter just quoted was written. Werferth was a Mercian, like Plegmund, the Archbishop of Canterbury, who also helped Alfred in his work of translation, and the scholars who have detected Mercian rather than Wessex expressions, cannot argue from the language where the work was performed, for as we have seen, the Court of Alfred, like the Court of Charlemagne, drew its scholars from all parts.

The book that gives us most of Alfred himself, though written by a monk, deals with secular history, and Alfred did not hesitate to add to it where he had knowledge, as of northern Europe, which the author did not possess. The author was a Spanish monk called Orosius, born at Tarragona late in the fourth century. He made himself a disciple of St Augustine at Hippo, and Augustine sent him on after a time to St Jerome with a letter of introduction which runs:

> Behold there has come to me a religious young man, in Catholic peace a brother, in age a son, in rank a co-presbyter, Orosius – of active talents, ready eloquence, ardent application, longing to be in God's house, a vessel useful for disproving false and destructive doctrines which have killed the souls of the Spaniards much more grievously than the sword of the barbarians their bodies. He has hastened to us from the ocean shore, expecting from a report, that

✝ ÐEOS BOC SCEAL TO WIOGORA CEASTRE ∴

ÆLFred kyning hateð gretan wærferð biscep his wordum luf
lice ⁊ freondlice; ⁊ ðe cyðan hate ðæt me com swiðe oft on ge
mynd hwelce wiotan iu wæron giond angel cynn, ægðer ge godcundra
hada ge woruldcundra; ⁊ hu gesæliglica tida ða wæron giond angel
cynn; ⁊ hu ða kyningas ðe ðone onwald hæfdon ðæs folces gode ⁊ his
ærend wrecum hyrsumedon; ⁊ hie ægðer ge hiora sibbe ge hiora
siodo ⁊ hiora onweald innan bordes gehioldon, ⁊ eac ut hiora
eðel gerymdon; ⁊ hu him ða speow ægðer ge mid wige ge mid wisdome;
⁊ eac ða godcundan hadas hu giorne hie wæron ægðer ge ymb lare
ge ymb liornunga; ge ymb ealle ða ðiowotdomas ðe hie gode scol
don; ⁊ hu man utan bordes wisdom ⁊ lare hieder on lond sohte; ⁊
hu we hy nu sceoldon ute begietan gif we hie habban sceoldon. Swa
clæne hio wæs oðfeallenu on angel cynne. ðæt swiðe feawa wæron
behionan humbre ðe hiora ðeninga cuðen understondan on eng
lisc, oððe furðum an ærend gewrit of lædene on englisc areccean.
⁊ ic wene ðæt noht monige begiondan humbre næren; swa
feawa hiora wæron ðæt ic furðum anne anlepne ne mæg
geðencean besuðan temese ða ða ic to rice feng; gode ælmih
tegum sie ðonc ðæt we nu ænigne onstal habbað lareowa; ⁊ for
ðon ic ðe bebiode. ðæt ðu do swa ic geliefe ðæt ðu wille, ðæt ðu ðe
ðissa woruld ðinga to ðæm geæmetige swa ðu oftost mæge, ðæt ðu
ðone wisdom ðe ðe god sealde ðær ðær ðu hiene befæstan mæge, befæste.

Hatton. 88.

he might learn from me whatever he wished of those matters he desired to know: but he has not reaped the fruit of his labour. First I desired him not to trust much to fame respecting me: next I taught him what I could; but what I could not, I told him where he might learn and I advised him to come to you. On which matter, having willingly and obediently acceded to my advice or command, I have asked him, on his coming from you, that he will take us on his way home.

St Jerome thanked St Augustine for sending him a copy of the book by so celebrated a man as Orosius whom he gladly welcomed. To have elicited at quite an early age such commendation from two of the leading Latin Doctors of the Church, was a high tribute which Orosius fully deserved. He had compiled a history of the world to support the thesis developed by St Augustine in his famous work *The City of God*. The central thesis of St Augustine was the contrast between the Christian society as it was beginning to flower into Christendom through the official conversion of the Roman Empire, and the heathen world full of demons and evil spirits, and the misfortunes natural to mankind in its fallen state. The monk Orosius consequently depicted the history of the world as far as he knew it, without sparing the horrors.

It is, indeed, always necessary to remember how much of the history that was written between the fourth century and the sixteenth was written in monasteries by men who had early in life renounced the wicked world. They were vividly conscious of the superiority of the ordered tranquility of their lives, tranquil so largely because they had flung away ambition, and the strain, the danger, the disappointments that were the common lot of people in the world outside, where the strong oppressed the weak, the rich the poor, and men cheated and fought, usually without success, to make their lives secure and prosperous. Monastic chronicles were the obvious place in which to record, like the log-book of a ship, every occurrence, with an assurance of continuity as a younger monk was set to understudy, and one day to take over from, an older monk. It is in this form that most of our knowledge of English history before the thirteenth century has come down to us. Very often, the verdict on a ruler was primarily determined by his attitude to the Church. If he protected and endowed the Church he was good, if he despoiled or overtaxed the Church, appropriating the incomes of vacant sees and recommending unworthy men for reasons of his own, he was bad. Over a century before Alfred's day, Charlemagne's grandfather, Charles Martel, or 'The Hammer', though he could claim to have saved Western Europe by halting the apparently irresistible advance of the Moors through Spain across the Pyrenees by his great victory at Poitiers, had a bad monastic press because he despoiled instead of endowing religious foundations; yet he despoiled them in the interest of a strong monarchy which was overwhelmingly in everybody's interest in a century when the Vikings from the north and the Saracens from the south penetrated all parts of Western Europe to destroy and loot.

Orosius wrote a work that survived because despite his cloistered life, he had a genuine intellectual curiosity, and gave his readers a great deal of new information. Alfred could not have picked a better book as a general history to make his subjects better-educated people. Orosius makes many curious mistakes which Alfred does not correct. For example, he begins with a description of the world as known to the Ancients, consisting of three parts, Asia, Europe and Africa, and divided by the river Tanais; at the end of his second geographical paragraph, after the statement that at this south-west end of Europe is Spain, ending with the island called Cadiz, where the Mediterranean flows into the ocean through the Pillars of Hercules, comes the assertion that in this same Mediterranean to the westward is Scotland, by which at that time was meant the island of Ireland. But the geography becomes, as might be expected, increasingly precise as it reaches the Near East, where the capital of the empire had been placed by Constantine. It is interesting that he gives the precedence to Asia, and only the second place to Europe, building his description round the course of the Rhine, and calling the whole of northern Europe Germany. (It puzzled Alfred very much, watching smaller rivers flow into the Thames, and the Thames into the sea at London how it was they kept up their perpetual flow of water, and his explanation was that they kept their identities and made their way back from the ocean under the earth till they rejoined their original source and started their round all over again.)

hasdrubal hisne selfne asealde
hys pif mid hisse þ·am·ý un·ú· hie selfe for behinde fon
þæs syrninyg deaðe syrypia het ealle þa buryg for byrnan
· and ælcne hiðe stan to beatan þ· hie to nanú· þealle riþþan
5 ne meahton· ·and burg hime þeard barn· ·xvii· dagas ymb
dcc· pintra þæs þe heðurh ge timbread pæs· þa þes þrid
de sepin ge lidad punica ·and romana on þam ge lidan syape
þæs þe hit sy on sunnan pæs þeh þe romane hæfdon þilong
sum ge mot emb þæt hpæðer him pæd læse þehe þehie þa
10 buryg mid ealle for dydon þ· hie ariþþan on þa healfe ·frid
hæfdon· þehi hie storidan forlæten to þon þ· him sepin þet þo
nan on poce forþon þe hie ondredon gif hie hpillum ne þun
nen þ· hie to pase ærlapoðen ·and a earpoðen· ·spa þ· top pomanú·
nu syt lið þearh riþþan ge tu sith dom pas cpæð oposiur
15 þ· ge lop siyria reld pihta hpi stan forlusan þop siyria se pin
na· ·and toppe hpæt sciþes foron ge rindon nu utan pæste
· and innan hlæne· ·and toppe reld ran pæs hon utan hlæne ·and innan
pæste foron ge moðye· ·and sciðes · Ionax che hu nys le þa
hpile bið þe le harþorid sy pæse bitan þæt le min ge spinc a
20 miþþe· hit bið eac to þinlic· þæt mon heard lice mide þone
hnt stan mealm stan ærþi þam þ· he þince þone roelestan
hpæt stan on to ge pittean ne· spa þon isy me nu spiðe earpede
hisgu mod tou hpættan ne· nu hit nappir nyre bion norce app
ne heard ...
·I· Cpæð oposiur hpæt se pomana gelp sy þost ys for þon
26 þehie monega polc ofgi punnan· and monge synin gar be
foran hisra quumphan oft pædlice dyson· þæt sindon
pagodan gda þehie ealne fore gelp að· ge licost þam þehie nu
cpeðen þ· þa cida him anú· ge reald e piþon· and nesten eallum
30 polcum· de þæs hieht· se pinne on stan tu þa þon pisten hie

Two pages from Orosius's history of the
world in the original manuscript, of which
eighty leaves survive. The figure kneeling is
St Matthew; the other evangelists are
represented by the ox of St Luke, the eagle of
St John and an *agnus dei*, instead of a lion, for
St Mark. The rectangle with leaf ornament is
inscribed VINEA DOMINI.

It is in the monk's description of northern Europe that Alfred inserted what he had learned from a northern merchant called Ohthere, who told Alfred about his voyages in the far north:

Ohthere told his lord King Alfred that he dwelt northmost of all the Northmen. He said that he dwelt in the land to the north-ward, along the West-Sea; he said, however, that the land is very long north from thence, but it is all waste, except in a few places, where the Fins here and there dwell, for hunting in the winter, and in the summer for fishing in that sea. He said that he was desirous to try, once on a time, how far that country extended due north, or whether anyone lived to the north of the waste. He then went due north along the country, leaving all the way the waste land on the right, and the wide sea on the left, for three days: he was as far north as the whale-hunters go at the farthest. Then he proceeded in his course due north, as far as he could sail within another three days; then the land there inclined due east, or the sea into the land, he knew not which but he knew that he there waited for a west wind, or a little north, and sailed then eastward along that land as far as he could sail in four days; then he had to wait for a due north wind because the land there inclined due south, or the sea in on that land, he knew not which; he then sailed along that coast due south, as far as he could sail in five days.

There lay a great river up in that land; they then turned up that river, because they durst not sail on by that river on account of hostility, because all that country was inhabited, on the other side of that river; he had not before met with any land that was inhabited since he came from his own home; but all the way he had waste land on his right, except fishermen, fowlers and hunters, all of whom were Fins, and he had constantly a wide sea to the left. The Beormas had well cultivated their country, but they did not dare to enter it; and the Terfinna land was all waste, except where hunters, fishers or fowlers had taken up their quarters. The Beormas told him many particulars both of their own land, and of the other lands lying around them; but he knew not what was true, because he did not see it himself; it seemed to him that the Fins and the Beormas spoke nearly one language.

He went thither chiefly, in addition to seeing the country, on account of the walrusses, because they have very noble bones in their teeth, some of those teeth they brought to the king: and their hides are good for ship-ropes. This whale is much less than other whales, it being not longer than seven ells; but in his own country is the best whale-hunting; there they are eight-and-forty ells long, and most of them fifty ells long; of these he said he and five others had killed sixty in two days. He was a very wealthy man in those possessions in which wealth consists, that is in wild deer. He had at the time he came to the king six hundred unsold tame deer. These deer they call rein-deer, of which there were six decoy rein-deer, which are very valuable among the Fins, because they catch the wild rein-deer with them. He was one of the first men in that country, yet he had not more than twenty horned cattle, and twenty sheep, and twenty swine, and the little he ploughed he ploughed with horses. But their wealth consists for the most part in the rent paid them by the Fins. That rent is in skins of animals, and birds' feathers and whalebone, and in ships' ropes made of whales' hides and of seals. Everyone pays according to his birth; the best-born, it is said, pay the skins of fifteen martens, and five rein-deers, and the bear's skin, ten ambers of feathers, a bear's or other's skin kyrtle, and two ship-ropes, each sixty ells long, made either of whale's hide or of seal's.

Another voyager whom Alfred inserts into his version of Orosius was a Dane, but with the Saxon name of Wulfstan, whose home was at Slesvig on the coast from which, in their day, the Angles, Saxons and Jutes had made their way to England. Wulfstan described to Alfred a voyage he had made round the Baltic Sea to discover where it led, and in it he gives a long and strange account of the Esthonians, and their curious burial habits, which obviously struck Alfred's imagination, and probably aroused his strong disapproval, seeing the importance he, like his father, attached to the right of a man to dispose of his possessions after his death as he himself chose. Wulfstan described how the Esthonians, having discovered how to make freezing mixture and ice, kept the bodies unburied for a month or more, before finally cremating them. In this interval they amused themselves by organising horse races from point to point, the points being piles of the dead man's possessions, growing in value as they were set up at an increasing distance from the house where his body lay. The value of what could thus be won was apparently such as to put a special price on the horses used for the purpose of these races. There is no mention of the dead man's family enjoying any rights of inheritance, and except that what happened was spun out over several weeks, it amounted to a man's seizing his neighbour's goods when that neighbour died.

As in all northern countries, fermented liquor was made from honey where grapes would not grow; mead is mentioned by Wulfstan as the drink of the poor, while the well-to-do apparently drank mares' milk, probably fermented *Kumiss*, and they did not appear to have ale.

We know that Offa had engaged in the export of cloth to the Carolingian Empire, the beginnings of what was to grow into a vast and profitable business, the export of English cloth and wool to the Low Countries. It may well be that Alfred had in his mind the possibilities of trading with northern Europe when he devotes so much attention to that part of the world and to the geography of what he termed 'Germania', for it is his information, not that of Orosius, which sets out where the different German tribes had their homes, and obviously Alfred had quite a clear idea about the northern mainland.

In addition to his own contributions, Alfred's translation gives us an insight into what an educated man of the ninth century might be expected to know. By that time the practice of dating our era *Anno Domini* from the Incarnation had taken root. But Orosius lived well before the change, and he reckons everything from what is to him the central date in history, the foundation of Rome in 753 BC. He opens his account by writing about Ninus, the founder of Nineveh, who is described as the first conqueror who introduced the habit of war as a rewarding pastime for kings, and taught the hitherto innocent Scythians who took to it with a vengeance, and from whom he eventually met his death. Orosius then comes down, picking his way among the dynasties and conquerors of Asia Minor, and getting ever nearer to the Romans who are already causing alarm before the emergence of Alexander the Great. There is then a curious biblical interpolation, an account of how Adam was created, full of good qualities, but instead of proceeding from Genesis into Old Testament history, Orosius abruptly switches his attention from the Garden of Eden to Romulus and Remus. From that point onwards, the story of Rome becomes, book by book, more and more the dominating theme, and in his fifth and sixth books he is describing chronologically the emergence and the generally brief reigns of the Roman emperors. Then, towards the end, when he comes to the rise of the Emperor Constantine, he is surprisingly unexcited at such a stupendous event. He briefly, and rather flatly, describes the persecution ordered by Galerius and Licinius, the war between them and Constantine, until Constantine took Licinius prisoner, and afterwards ordered him to be beheaded, and then succeeded to the whole Roman Empire. This sentence is followed immediately by one which says that in those days Arius, the Mass priest, fell into error concerning the right belief. In consequence of that crime there assembled 318 bishops at Nicaea in 325 AD to confute and excommunicate him. You would think that this might be sufficiently interesting to deserve development, but Orosius has finished with the first great council. He comes back immediately to political history, writing:

> In those days Constantine slew his son Crispin, and Licinius, his sister's son, so that no one knew what their sin was save him alone. After that he subjected to himself many nations that before were unsubdued by the Romans, and commanded a city to be built in Greece, and commanded it to be named from himself Constantinople. He first of men commanded churches to be built, and that every heathen temple should be closed. He died thirty-one years after he had the Empire in a villa near the city of Nicomodaea.

The world of Orosius is a world in which the Catholic Church, which shines through every page of Pope Gregory's writing and rulings, is not mentioned, and if we remember that his theme was the evils of paganism, we begin to understand why. He held that Rome had survived because God had protected the city because of the Christians in it, so that the Caesars were still ruling and the Goths had been repulsed.

> This I say now because I am desirous that those may understand who inveigh against these times of our Christianity. What mercy there was after Christianity was, and how manifold was the world's calamity before that was; and also that they may know how fitly our God in these early times established them, and turns every power and every realm to his will; how like a beginning these two cities [Babylon and Rome] had, and how like were their days, everything good and then evil; but the ends of their power, however, were very unlike; for the Babylonians with their manifold wickednesses and sinful lusts, together with their king, who living without any repentance, so that they would not amend before God had humbled them with the greatest ignominy when he

HIERONIMVS ROMAE CONGREGAVIRRA · ⳨ · IRVSALEM MEORREAE LEGIS MONOALTI ·

AS TOEMIO SE MENOM PAVLE DIVINA SS A IIEO · VTAPA TAIT · RONO EVLTVS VBIQVE DO

IERONIMVS TRANSLATIO SSO QVAE TRANSTVLIT ALM · OLLIS HIC TRIBVIT QVIS EA CON POSVIT ·

deprived them both of their king and of their power. But the Romans, with their Christian king, served God, so that he granted them both their king and their power. Therefore may those moderate their speech who are adversaries of Christianity if they will recollect the uncleanliness of their forefathers, their calamitous wars, their manifold dissensions, and their cruelty, which they had to guard, and also between themselves, so that they would perform no mercy before the atonement of Christianity came, which they now vehemently reproach.

It is interesting to know that Alfred's taste in choosing Orosius for his subjects was also the popular choice of Europe for centuries. Irrelevant as the basic argument became as the city of Rome passed through so many vicissitudes, it is a proof of the continued prevalence of the great idea of Roman Empire that the book was so constantly copied and re-copied until printing was invented in the middle of the fifteenth century, when it became one of the first books to be printed in Germany in 1471.

The third historical work which Alfred gave his subjects to supplement the *Anglo-Saxon Chronicle* and Orosius was an Anglo-Saxon translation of the Latin *Ecclesiastical History of the English Nation* from the pen of the Venerable Bede.

We have seen Alfred taking considerable liberties with Orosius in marked contrast to the respectful and indeed minute care he had shown towards the writings of Pope Gregory. With Bede he acts even more freely, omitting about a third of the work. He leaves out all the seventh century controversies about the date of Easter which had divided Celtic and Saxon Christians so deeply. Where Bede has been following Orosius, Alfred leaves those pages out. In the great dearth of contemporary narratives about seventh- and eighth-century Europe, Bede's *History* stands alone, but he died in 735, and posterity has never ceased to regret that Alfred, in translating it, did not continue it down to his own day, covering the hundred and fifty years about which our materials are woefully insufficient. Every now and then Asser gives us a glimpse of Alfred's conversation, as about Offa's wicked daughter (see p. 20), which shows how much he knew and how interested he was; but he left no proper record.

Bede tells in detail the story of the conversion of Ethelbert, the

King of Kent, who reigned for fifty-six years from 560 to 616, by the party of monks led by St Augustine whom Pope Gregory sent out from his own monastery on the Coelian Hill in Rome, the monastery that had been the home of his wealthy family before he and his mother devoted it to the service of religion. One of the great defects of those who wrote the lives of saints in the Dark Ages is their lack of scruple in improving episodes to make them more edifying, in showing great credulity because for them the more miraculous happenings there were, the better for everybody; but from these defects Bede is strikingly free, and although he was writing over a century after the events he was describing, he had talked with

The chair at Jarrow in which Bede passed most of his day, writing, meditating and teaching.

157

men much older than himself, which was one of the advantages
a young monk could enjoy, and some of these older men could
themselves remember the first missionaries and their immediate companions and disciples. There is no hagiography
about Bede's account of St Augustine of Canterbury, and his
work is all the more convincing on that account.

He shows St Augustine as a nervous monk, an Italian and
Roman, with the common view of his countrymen that the
further north a man goes from Rome, the further he is then
from civilisation, that north Gaul was more barbarous than
Provence which could rank with north Italy, and Britain more
barbarous than northern Gaul. When he reached Gaul, the
people there took pleasure in scaring him and his companions
with what they would meet if they crossed the Channel, so
that for a moment he turned back and had to be prodded by the
Pope to persevere. For his part, King Ethelbert was equally
apprehensive that these strangers might have magical arts at
their command, and insisted on meeting them in person in the
open air. St Augustine's nervousness was shared by his immediate companions and successors who, when they feared that
the men of Kent, led by Ethelbert's back-sliding son, were
giving up the Faith as the Saxons in Essex had done, both
Miletus and Lawrence, the one Bishop of London and the other
St Augustine's immediate successor at Canterbury, hastily with-
drew to Gaul. When Augustine formally met the bishops of the
Celtic or British Church, they attached immense importance
to whether he would stand up to receive them in a spirit of
Christian brotherhood, or remain seated to assert his authority
in the Roman tradition. He remained seated, and the meeting
was fruitless. All this Bede tells in a restrained and objective way,
and then he tells of the later missionaries who converted the
Mercians, of St Chad and St Birinus, and of the way the Pope,
whose authorisation they needed, respected the territorial rights
of the missionaries already established, and made it a condition
that the later missionaries should break new ground. Then he
tells the dramatic story of the Greek St Theodore of Tarsus. He
was the prior in a monastery near Naples whose abbot was
selected by the Pope to fill the distant see of Canterbury in
Britain. The abbot, who was probably very comfortable where
he was, refused the adventurous appointment, and so his prior

Incipit prephatio vene
rabilis BEDE presbiteri
in vitam beati patris
CVTHBERTI Lindisfarnensis.

DOMINO AC BEATISSIMO
patri EADFRIDO EPO. & oi
om̄ congregationi fratrum̄ q̄
in Lindisfarnensi insula
xp̄o deserviunt. beda fidel
ur cservus salutē. Quia ius
sistis dilectissimi. ut libro quē
de vita beatę memorię patris n̄ri
CVTHBERTI vivo rogatu coposui. p̄fatione aliq̄ in fron
te iuxta morē p̄sigerē. p̄quā legentib̄ ynuisit & uię
voluntatis desideriū. & obedientionis n̄ę parte assensio
fr̄na claresceret. p̄lacuit in capite p̄fationis & vob
q̄nostis ad memoriā revocare. & eis q̄ ignorant hęc
forte legentib̄ notū facere. q̄a nec sine certissima in
q̄sitione rerū gestarū. aliqd de tanto viro scribe. nec tan
de ea que scripserā sine subtili examinatione testiū
in dubiois pssit cuiscribenda qbdā dare p̄supsisse.
qn potiꝰ p̄imo diligent exordiū. p̄gressū. & tmimū glo
sissime cū sationis acuire. illa ab his q̄ noverant · in
vestigasse. Quorus etiā nomina in ipso libro aliquoti
ens ob certā cognite veritatis inditū apponenda iu
dicavi. & sic demum ad scedulas manum mittere
incipio. At digesto opuscula. sed ad huc in scedulis
retento. Ut frequent & reverentissimo fr̄ n̄o heresfrido
presbitero huc advenienta. & aliis qui diutiꝰ cuui
ro di cū sati. vitā illiꝰ optime noverant. que scrip
si legenda atq̄ ex tempore p̄storia retractanda. ac n̄
nulla ad arbitriū eoꝝ pptiu videbant: sedulꝰ em
davi Sicq̄ ablatis omnib̄. scrupulois ambagib̄ ad
purū. certā veritatis indagine simplicib̄ explici
tā sermonib̄ cōmdare membranulis. atq̄ advitę
q̄q̄ fratris p̄sentiā asportare curavi: quatinus

was chosen in his place. Theodore was not a young man, already old for those days, but he came to England and did an immense work in establishing an ecclesiastical unity which prepared the ground for the political unity that was to be achieved much later, for Theodore was ruling the Church of Wessex and Mercia two hundred years before Alfred was ruling the State.

Bede was a Northumbrian, and his life coincided with the Northumbrian pre-eminence among the Anglo-Saxon kingdoms, but by Alfred's time, as we have seen, the Danes, Angles, Saxons and Jutes were already conscious that they together made up the English nation who figured in the title of Bede's work, while the other half of his title, *Ecclesiastical History*, kept in the forefront of their minds that the most important thing in their lives was that they were Christians, members of the Catholic Church under the Pope in Rome. When Bede was next translated into English, it was some seven hundred years after Alfred's Anglo-Saxon translation. It was translated by a Catholic exile in the Low Countries in the early years of Elizabeth's reign to show the English what the religion of their ancestors had been, not the Protestant Christianity imported from Germany or Switzerland by the returned Marian exiles, but a religion centred around the Mass which was then under such violent attack.

The last of the books of enduring fame which Alfred selected for translation was something very different. The *Consolation of Philosophy* by Boethius is a work written by a Roman under sentence of death around 520. It is a book with an extraordinary history of sustained popularity all through the Middle Ages, comparable to the popularity of Gregory's *Pastoral Care* or Orosius's *History*. There was a good deal of confusion whether Boethius, whose full name was Anicius Manlius Severinus, is to be identified with a Christian martyr St Severinus. The *Consolation* is with Gregory and Bede in Alcuin's list of the library at York, and yet it is not theological or devotional, but philosophical, a book a Greek philosopher might have written before Christ. It is full of reflections on the transience of human things, and the vicissitudes of individual fortunes, and how the wise man, listening to the voice of Philosophy, will accept good and evil fortune with an equable mind. Probably most of those who cherished the book, including Alfred, assumed Boethius was a Christian, and certainly there is nothing incompatible

160

with the Christian doctrine in the *Consolation*. It is only strange that Christ is nowhere mentioned, that the whole feeling of the work is in a different world from a work written in comparable circumstances, St Thomas More's *Dialogue of Comfort in Tribulation*. But Alfred put much of himself into the translation of the poems with which the book is studded, and it probably appealed to him since he had himself known great alternations of fortune, great adversity and, for his times, great prosperity. All the same, it remains rather a strange choice for the common reader to have figured so early in the first half-dozen books translated or projected, for what we have should not be taken as more than a beginning of what Alfred, had he lived longer, would have given his countrymen who did not read Latin.

The *Consolation* has a special interest for us because from the nature of the subject matter, when Alfred makes an interpolation or a gloss of his own, it is personal and revealing. Thus when Boethius writes: 'Thou knowest that ambition never was my mistress, though I did desire materials for carrying out my task', Alfred adds:

> Which task was that I should virtuously and fittingly administer the authority committed to me. Now no man can administer government unless he have fit tools and the raw material to work upon ... and a king's raw materials and instruments of rule are a well-peopled land, and he must have men of prayer, men of war and men of work ... without these tools he cannot perform any of the tasks entrusted to him.

Similarly the poem which he prefixes to the translation sheds light on his idea of Christendom. Boethius was pledged to the service of the Goth Theodoric, but he hankered after the restoration of the Roman Emperor Justinian in Constantinople. Despite the immense importance Alfred in his laws attached to loyalty due from all men to their superiors, by ordinary men to their thanes and by thanes to their king, he applauds Boethius because he considers the Greek, as he terms the Byzantine Emperor, the true representative of Constantine and the Christian Empire by contrast with the Goth.

Later in the book, Alfred says: 'My will was to live worthily as long as I live, and after my life to leave, to them that should come after, my memory in good works.' His translation is

ARDENTI CANCRI FERT IUL AUSTRUM
DIES XXX · LUNA · XXX ·

		F	G		IVL Caius et uictor gaudent iam sorte kalende.
XIX					
VIII		k	F A	VI N	Marcianus nonis insenis atq: processus.
	I C	G B	V N	Quinis narratur thome translatio sca.
XVI	I H	C	IIII N	Transfertur quadris martinus & ordine compus.
V	I D	III N	Trinis uinonis transfertur corpus agathe.
	O D M k	F	II N	Octauas colimus pridias exordine nonas.
XIII	I	NON	Honarumque die moelruen conscendit ingehram.
II	H M	G	VIII ID	Cesaree paritur procobus idibus octo.
	U E	H A	VII ID	Septenas retinet faustinus nomine ses.
X	O O	B	VI ID	Idibus insenis frm iam passio septem.
	A P	C	V ID	Quinis transfertur benedictus nomine ses.
XVIII	A F	Q D	IIII ID	Idibus inquadris agatha iam fulserat orbi.
VII	B R	E	III ID	Idibus en micuit sesque serapio trinis.
	S	F	II ID	Idus per pridias ustus deponitur almus.
XV	E G C	G	IDVS	Idibus exiuit florentius arbiter aruis.
IIII	U	A	XVII kt	ABS Atq: ualentinus denis septemq: kldis.
	D A	B	XVI kt	piana fulgens denis seuasq: kalendis.
XII	I H	B C	XV kt	QUINDECIMIS Scandit sol ardens terga leonis.
I	E C	D	XIIII kt	Denis & quadris arsenus & rusticus equant.
	D E	XIII kt	Tres decimis hausit uulmarus pocula uirg.
IX	O I E	F	XII kt	Bisenis uirgo pausauit praxidis alma.
	F	G	XI kt	Undecimis maria transiuit limina moras.
XVII	G G A	X	kt	Rite apollonaris ses denisque kalendis.
VI	U k	H S	VIIII kt	Iacobus octo dni fraterque kalendis.
	I	VIII kt	Felix & iuliane saturnine repausas.
XIIII	k	VII kt	At simeon senis dormit pausatq: kldis.
III	A A	L	VI kt	Armonicus pastor samson quinisq: kldis.
	k	V kt	E austinus & felix simpliciusq: beatis.
XI	k	IIII kt	Consecrat ternas abdo senesq: kldas.
XIX	B B	O A	III kt	Germanus meruit pridias gaudere kalendas.
	B	II kt	

made the vehicle for a number of moral precepts against idleness and the desire for a soft life, and how important is the good intention with which work is performed, more important than the measure of success or fame, and that a good reputation is a better possession than any wealth. It is Alfred who puts into the mouth of Philosophy the observation: 'When I with my servants mount aloft, then do we look down upon the stormy world, even as the eagle when he soars above the clouds in stormy weather, so that the storms cannot hurt him.'

The last of Alfred's works is in some ways the most personal, for it is an anthology of various writings which appealed to him, foremost among them part of St Augustine's *Soliloquies*, into the second of which Alfred puts a good many of his own ideas, paraphrasing freely. He then goes on with another extract from St Augustine, this time from his epistle to Pauline on the Vision of God, and from perhaps the most famous of St Augustine's works *The City of God*. Alfred also includes some writings of St Gregory, his dialogue dealing with the life of St Benedict and his *Moralia*. To the whole work he added a moving preface on the metaphor of the builder in wood who selects his trees, fells them and fashions them into blocks and then builds with them, saying:

> Nor did I ever bring any burden home without longing to bring home the whole wood, if that might be; for in every tree I saw something of which I had need at home. Wherefore I exhort every one who is strong and has many wains that he direct his steps to the same wood where I cut the props. Let him there get him others, and load his wains with fair twigs, that he may weave thereof many a goodly wain, and set up many a noble house, and build many a pleasant town, and dwell there in mirth, and ease, both summer and winter, as I could never do hitherto. But He who taught me to love that wood, He may cause me to dwell more easily, both in this transitory dwelling ... while I am in the world, and also in the eternal home which He has promised us. ...

While Alfred drew on the Latin Fathers of the Church, St Gregory and St Augustine, or on the Roman senator Boethius, he did not succeed, as far as we know, in securing from Rome any learned men to come and work in England. He brought from Germany a man known as John the Old Saxon whom he

OPPOSITE The month of June from the Saxon calendar; loading a wain with wood.

put in charge of the monastery he attempted to found on the Isle of Athelney, obviously in thanksgiving, for it was at Athelney that he had touched the lowest depths of his military misfortunes. But the foundation did not prosper. Perhaps it was overshadowed by Glastonbury, a few miles away, which had escaped being ravished by the Danes. More probably it failed because he had to import most of the monks from the Continent, and they never settled down under their German superior in what cannot have been then a very attractive part of the country; indeed, it seems they murdered him.

Alfred's most notable acquisition came to him from much nearer home, from Rheims, and the letter still exists which he exchanged with Fulk, Archbishop of Rheims, by which Alfred traded hunting dogs for an elderly and scholarly monk by name Grimbald. Fulk replies with the habitual Frankish arrogance. The Franks, who had entered Gaul about the same time as the Saxons entered England, found a much more civilised society, for Gaul had been Romanised much more thoroughly than Britain, and the Frankish chiefs were much more consciously trying to inherit Roman dignities, taking possession of Roman cities, where the Saxons in the middle of the fifth and sixth centuries tended to avoid the Roman towns in Britain and to make their own settlements. There were exceptions to this such as Canterbury, London, Winchester and York, but in general the Romanised Britons represented a smaller, simpler and more primitive society than the Gallo-Romans, even in the north of Gaul. So we find Fulk writing rather haughtily, contrasting the way St Remigius, after whom Rheims was named,

> ... had redeemed the Franks from manifold error and taught them to know the worship of the one true God, so that the English may beg to receive such a man from his see and teaching, through whom it may learn to guard against superstition, cut off superfluities, and to extirpate anything harmful springing from ancient use and barbarian custom, and walking through the Lord's field they learn to pluck the fruit and avoid the snake.

And he goes on:

> Certainly, St Augustine, the first bishop of your people, sent to you by the Blessed Gregory, your apostle, neither could demonstrate in a short time all the decrees, the apostolic ordinances, nor

The only surviving Anglo-Saxon wooden church, heavily restored, is at St Andrew, Greensted, Essex, where tree trunks have been split and arranged upright, their flat surfaces forming the inner wall of the nave. Up to the Norman Conquest even great churches were sometimes built in wood, not stone.

Anglo-Saxon Churches

The study of Anglo-Saxon architecture is based on ecclesiastical buildings, since churches have proved more enduring than dwellings. Altogether there are several hundred churches still containing varying amounts of Anglo-Saxon stonework. In Alfred's reign most churches were built of wood but stone had been used as far back as the seventh century. The structure was usually simply a nave and chancel, both rectangular.

LEFT Much of St John's Church at Escomb, County Durham, was built of Roman masonry in the seventh to eighth centuries. The larger windows are of a later date but the smaller are original.
ABOVE The interior of St John's; the central window on the right is original.

LEFT The construction of stone churches seems often to have followed the way in which wooden churches were built. The pilaster strips on the tower of All Saints, Earls Barton, Northamptonshire, are imitations of the Saxon timber constructions.

RIGHT Saxon windows at Holy Trinity Church, Deerhurst, Gloucestershire.

wished suddenly to burden a rude and barbarous people with new and unknown laws; for he knew how to have regard for their weakness, and to say with the Apostle, as it were to little ones in Christ, I give you milk to drink, not meat.

And he went on to rub in how the rearing from barbaric and savage beginnings to divine knowledge required good mentors, and that the Church had always been apostolic; and so he came very long-windedly to the point for which Alfred was waiting, that because of the splendid present Alfred had sent, Fulk was not only warmly praising the glorious and Christian King of the English but sending him Grimbald, for whom he had particularly asked, as a man fully worthy to be made a bishop, and that he himself wished to consecrate Grimbald, but instead he had decided to send Grimbald to Alfred to make him a bishop with the approval of the local magnates in England, so that he would be more acceptable.

This letter has been challenged with the argument that it assumes throughout that Grimbald was to be a bishop, whereas in fact he never was. He does not seem to have had any clear and big promotion while Alfred lived. He was a monk of St Bertin, an important monastery in Flanders of which Fulk, Archbishop of Rheims, was also a monk, and of which Fulk was acting as abbot in addition to his archbishopric, and apparently contrary to the wishes of the community who had wanted Grimbald to be their abbot when Alfred's request came. He was evidently a notable scholar; he is thanked, along with Plegmund, the Archbishop of Canterbury, and Asser, for his help in Alfred's translations of St Gregory's *Pastoral Care*, and it may well be that in the last decade of Alfred's life he valued Grimbald too much to part with him.

Perhaps deterred by the failure to found a monastery at Athelney, Alfred moved very cautiously in his larger ambition of a monastery in Winchester near to the cathedral, but inhabited by monks, whereas the cathedral itself was served by secular canons who lived much less strictly. The New Minster which became famous as Hyde Abbey was not complete when Alfred died, but it was almost complete, and one of the first acts of his son Edward was to establish it and to make Grimbald abbot; though he did not live very long, Grimbald achieved a

OPPOSITE St Mark from a sumptuous manuscript of the Rheims school, first half of the ninth century. The floating draperies suggest figures set in motion by the breath of God.

Examples of Anglo-Saxon stone-carving:
ABOVE A saint in St Mary's, Sompting.
ABOVE RIGHT An angel from St Lawrence's, Bradford-on-Avon.
BELOW RIGHT An eagle from All Saints', Brixworth.
FAR RIGHT A cross shaft standing in St Peter's, Codford.

A bronze seal-die which probably belonged to Ethelwald, bishop of Dunwich, in the mid-ninth century. The die is decorated with a floriated cross and the seal with animal heads.

place in the English calendar of saints as neither Asser nor John the Old Saxon succeeded in doing. Historically Grimbald's name was closely associated with the tradition that Alfred interested himself in Oxford, and that there was a sufficient centre of learning there for him to seek to strengthen it. University College, in particular, long claimed Alfred as its founder.

The case against Alfred's having any connection with Oxford rests chiefly on the view that there was nothing that could be called a university before the twelfth century, and that there were no colleges before late in the thirteenth. It also rests on the argument that nothing is said about Oxford until Camden's edition of Asser's *Life* which appeared in 1603.

On the other hand it does not always follow that interpolations are baseless. The Oxford interpolation, if it had been devised merely to demonstrate the vastly superior antiquity of Oxford over Cambridge, could have been much more direct, making Alfred a munificent founder or re-founder. What it in fact does is to say that Grimbald went to Oxford and was not welcomed by the learned clerks of the place. Grimbald was then an old man, probably very conscious of being somebody whose opinions ought to be heard with respect as representing the Carolingian renaissance, for he had begun his monastic life when the abbot of St Bertin's was himself a son of Charlemagne. Grimbald was said to have founded the church of St Peter in the East between what were later to be New College and Queen's College, and to have been buried there. Higden, in his *Polychronicum* of 1363 makes the earliest reference to Alfred actually founding faculties of the liberal arts at Oxford. This is generally accepted as certainly an anachronism since there were no faculties of arts before the twelfth century. But Grimbald's undoubted connection with Oxford makes it reasonable to think that there was some little learning there which Alfred may have encouraged, even though no-one from Oxford is thanked for helping in the King's literary projects.

What is certain about Grimbald is that he did not become a bishop. There is indeed some mystery about Alfred's attitude to episcopal appointments for, as we have seen, no sooner was he dead than his son Edward received a highly censorious communication from Rome, drawing attention to the number of vacant sees at his accession. It may well have been that even at this early date, it had become customary for the king to take the revenue of sees during the vacancies, a bad custom as a result of which, throughout the Middle Ages, the see of Canterbury was kept vacant for one year out of every three.

5 The End of the Reign

and Alfred's Later Fame

PREVIOUS PAGES
The front and back of the
Alfred Jewel show the
exquisite workmanship of
which the Saxons were
capable. Asser says Alfred
laid aside one sixth of the
revenues of the kingdom
to pay 'artificers' but the
Alfred Jewel is the only
survival of his expenditure,
found at Athelney in the
seventeenth century. The
base is in the shape of a
boar's head with a hollow
snout and may have fitted
on a pointer. The jewel is
made of rock crystal over
cloisonné enamel set
in gold.

OPPOSITE The *Lindisfarne
Gospels* were written and
illuminated by Edfrith,
Bishop of Lindisfarne
(698–721) in the
combination of Celtic and
Anglo-Saxon style known
as Hiberno-Saxon, but
with some influence from
Mediterranean naturalism.
The Carpet page
illustrated here is
composed of interlaced
animals typical of
Anglo-Saxon style.

SCHOLARS ARE IN GENERAL AGREED that Asser wrote his *Life*
in 892 or 893, and therefore he tells us nothing of the last
peaceful years of the reign when the shadow of the Danes had
lifted after 896, or of the triumphant end of Alfred's last campaign, nor does the *Anglo-Saxon Chronicle* say more than that
many of those he had gathered round him died in these last
years, mentioning among them, rather curiously, an *ealdorman*
of Essex, whose rank was perhaps honorary after Essex had
been conceded to Guthrum. William of Malmesbury gives us
one glimpse of the King in his last years, being as pleased with
his attractive and promising grandson, Athelstan, with studious
as well as martial inclinations, as his own father Ethelwulf had
been with him, and decorating the future king with a scarlet
cloak, a jewelled belt and a Saxon sword with a golden scab-
bard. This is in keeping with what Asser tells us of Alfred's
sustained interest in jewelled ornaments, of which a dramatic
discovery near Athelney in 1683 produced striking proof, the
famous Alfred Jewel, now in the Ashmolean Museum at
Oxford and reproduced in this volume. As it has no trace of a
fastening it seems more likely that it was the crown of a writing
instrument such as the King would have constantly needed,
rather than a brooch or clasp. When Parliament seized the
Crown jewels from Charles I, at the top of the inventory was
the golden crown of King Alfred, studded with emeralds.

The great King died at Winchester while still in his early
fifties, but, as we may well imagine, older than his years from
all the stresses and strains he had undergone, and the ceaseless
activity which he laid down for himself. He left a will, an
elaborate document making extensive provision for the members of the royal House, for nephews as well as for his own
children. These nephews were the sons of brothers older than
Alfred. One of them made an unsuccessful attempt to supplant
Edward the Elder as Alfred's successor, but the *Witanagemot*
was well satisfied that Edward, in over ten years as his father's
lieutenant, had proved his worthiness to succeed. Alfred refers
back to his grandfather, Egbert, and his father, Ethelwulf, who
had both made detailed wills, leaning more to the spear side
than the spindle side of the family, as Alfred phrased it. Alfred
shared their conviction that the men of the royal House
must take precedence over the women because of the greater

The Minster Lovell Jewel constructed
similarly to the Alfred Jewel
but perhaps slightly later in date.

The Fuller Brooch, a ninth-century
silver ornament bearing symbols
of the five senses.

responsibilities they were likely to have to carry. But he forgot none of his children, and he left his widow three royal villas of particular interest: Wantage, his birthplace, which remained a royal possession into Plantagenet times; nearby Lambourn, by the site of his first great victory; and Ethandune, the scene of his most decisive triumph. He left Lewisham to his youngest daughter who had married the Count of Flanders, and it passed into the possession of a convent in Ghent. This seems to have been the kind of event Alfred was anxious to avoid, for he left instructions that the menfolk of his House were to buy out the womenfolk if occasion arose.

The impression his will makes is that the King of Wessex was very well off, and that, probably thanks to Egbert, the King had large personal possessions in addition to the lands formally assigned for the upkeep of the Crown. There are personal legacies to men like Plegmund, Archbishop of Canterbury, and there are humane provisions for the bondmen and those tied to the land, that they were to be free if they chose to go to another master and another estate, and there was to be no question of indemnification. It sounds as though this concession would have been primarily prejudicial to his son and heir, but Alfred took special care to see that his successor was strongly placed economically. He left £200 for Masses for his own and his father's souls, divided into four among the Mass-priests of the kingdom, the distressed poor, God's poor servants and the church at Winchester in which his body was to lie.

The *Chronicle* is content to record his death prosaically enough, but it was not a prosaic interment. The New Minster was not ready and he was buried in the old, and when a year or two later, the New Minster, soon to be Hyde Abbey, was ready, his body was transferred there, apparently with the full acquiescence of the canons of the Old Minster because, they said, he troubled them by appearing at night and walking in their cloisters in a way that much alarmed them. At the Reformation, when Hyde Abbey like all other religious houses was suppressed and then despoiled, the tombs of the Saxon kings were not spared. Some of the bones were later gathered into wooden caskets and placed above the chancel in Winchester Cathedral, but all mixed up. There they remain.

Alfred had looked forward to death because of his intense

OPPOSITE The *Chi Rho* page of the *Lindisfarne Gospels* shows St Matthew's Gospel at chapter one, verse eighteen. The great initials *Chi* and *Rho* are the first two letters of Christ in Greek.

An ivory panel from Winchester carved about fifty years after Alfred's death. The figures have much in common with the angels at Bradford-on-Avon (see page 171) and are probably similar to the fine carving of Alfred's reign, none of which survives.

intellectual curiosity, as he showed in the concluding sentence of his *Commonplace Book*, when he wrote: 'Therefore it seems to me a very foolish man, and very wretched, who will not increase his understanding while he is in the world, and ever wish and long to reach that endless life where all shall be made clear.'

For a man so busy with government, including the problem of defence against great difficulties, who lived up to Thomas Jefferson's maxim that it is wonderful how much we may do provided we are always doing something, it is striking how great a place Alfred made for prayer and the formal offices, the *Opus Dei* of the Catholic Church, as he had grown acquainted with them in his boyhood visits to Rome. His invention of a primitive way of recording time by indented candles which would mark the passage of time and lead by a fuse from one candle to another so that six could span the twenty-four hours of the day, and his device of finely-sliced white ox-horn panels in lanterns protecting the candle-flame, were used to ensure that his time was spent to the best advantage and with many hours for prayer as well as for business and sociability. To the medieval chroniclers who wrote about him, all this seemed natural enough, as did his devotion to the relics of saints, or his alms-giving, even the sending of alms as far afield as India, and his donation in response to the begging of the Patriarch of Jerusalem. Alfred's religious devoutness towards the set prayers of the Church made less appeal in later centuries, and Milton, when he wrote a history of England before the Norman Conquest, did not hesitate to share the view the Saxons themselves had held, that the Danish successes were often a punishment for Saxon wrong-doing, only Milton included among the wrong-doing what he saw as the superstitions of the Catholic faith which met him on every page of the chronicles which were his sources.

Alfred spent much of his time in the last years of his life at or near Winchester. The Saxons avoided the old Roman cities, but the Minster and the New Minster which Alfred planned were strong attractions. It is now generally agreed that it is anachronistic to talk of Winchester as having been the capital of Wessex in the sense in which Westminster and London would become the capital under Edward the Confessor. The seat of government was wherever the Wessex king chose to be. He had

Two objects from the hoard of ninth-century metalwork found at Trewhiddle in Cornwall: LEFT A silver chalice of which the inside was originally gilded. RIGHT A silver scourge attached to a head made of blue glass with white veining. It is the only object of its kind known from early Christian Europe and probably had a ceremonial use.

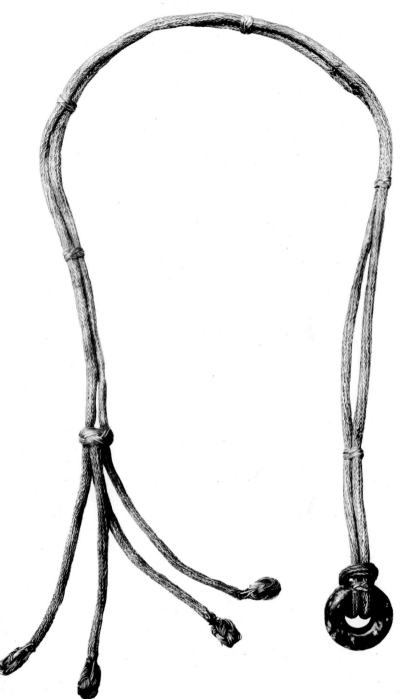

a number of royal *vills* or estates, and he went from one to another. But Winchester was geographically convenient. The king residing there could reach the sea or Kent or the West of England rapidly enough. It was a strongly fortified *burh*, but it was primarily the chief see of Wessex, and round Winchester Cathedral, with learned men like Grimbald at hand, Alfred continued to organise studies, and made it plain that regard for study was expected. For all his affability, he inspired awe, and Asser gives a touching picture of how, after they had been scolded by Alfred for, as he put it, neglecting the studies and labours of the wise, and had been commanded to do better, elderly men would tremble and turn all their thoughts to the study of justice, so that

> ... wonderful to say, almost all his earls, prefects and officers though unlearned from their cradles, were sedulously bent upon acquiring learning, choosing rather laboriously to acquire the knowledge of a new discipline than lose their functions; but if any one of them, from old age or slowness of talent was unable to make progress in liberal studies, he commanded his son if he had one or one of his kinsmen, or, if there was no other person to be had, his own free man or servant, whom he had some time before advanced to the office of reading, to recite Saxon books before him night and day, whenever he had any leisure, and they lamented with deep sighs in their inmost hearts that in their youth they had never attended to such studies; and they blessed the young men of our days who happily could be instructed in the liberal arts, while they execrated their own lot, that they had not learned these things in their youth, and now, when they are old and wishing to learn them they are unable.

The fruits of this were to come only with the next generation. It is not fanciful to trace the first origins of the great monastic revival led by St Dunstan and St Ethelwold to this compulsory culture instituted at Alfred's Court. His son Edward the Elder could not withstand his father's determination, and he created out of the vast Sherborne diocese the see of Wells in Somerset, a county for which he seems to have had a special fondness, and when Plegmund died Edward chose the bishop of this new see for promotion to Canterbury. This bishop, Adhelm by name, was the uncle of St Dunstan. His successor at Wells, Wulfheim, also went from Wells to Canterbury, and then the new Bishop

of Wells was another uncle of Dunstan who encouraged the youth (who was much taunted by his contemporaries for his studiousness) to enter the cloister at Glastonbury. Dunstan's chief lieutenant, St Ethelwold, was born at Winchester of parents connected with the Court, and he was soon drawn into the influence of the see of Wells and the abbey of Glastonbury six miles away. He ended his life as bishop of his native town, bringing the monks of Abingdon, where he had been abbot, to replace the canons of the cathedral.

As we have seen, Edward also completed Alfred's plans for a new Minster at Hyde Abbey. It became a great Saxon monastery, so Saxon that at the time of the Norman Conquest the abbot was Harold's uncle, and he led twelve of his younger and stronger monks onto the battlefield at Hastings. There they were slain to a man and the monastery severely penalised by William of Normandy. The Conqueror moved into Winchester and kept his royal treasure there, partly for its convenience for the New Forest to be the royal hunting-ground, but also no doubt to dominate it, lest it should become a centre of Saxon disaffection.

The only successful foundation in Alfred's own lifetime was a convent for women at Shaftesbury, of which he made one of his daughters the abbess. This prospered from the first, and when Shaftesbury became the scene of the treacherous murder of Alfred's great-great-grandson by his stepmother (who wanted to clear the way for her own son, Ethelred, to become king while still a boy), a cult of the murdered King Edward sprang up which brought pilgrims to Shaftesbury seeking miraculous favours at his shrine.

OPPOSITE A page from the *Benedictional of St Ethelwold*, illustrating the Annunciation. It shows the height of lavishness reached in the Winchester school of manuscript illumination in the tenth century. The Winchester style is noted for its vivid blending of naturalism and stylised ornamentation, its gracious figures and delicate colouring.

To gauge the full measure of Alfred's political achievement, it is necessary to look ahead to the reigns of his son and grandsons. Then we understand how completely the royal dynasty of Wessex was established as the dynasty of England. For most of Alfred's own reign the Severn Valley and west Mercia may be considered as almost part of Wessex, with the division of England between the south-west under Saxon rule and the north-east under Danish rule. The broad line of the Peace of Wedmore was steadily eroded as the Saxons pushed north-east to bring the rest of Mercia under Edward the Elder. When he

died in 925, although there were large Danish settlements in Lincolnshire, Norfolk and Suffolk, and in Essex, yet England south of the River Trent looked to the Wessex kings, and Edward's son and heir, Athelstan, starting from this large and solid base, extended his authority over Yorkshire and Northumberland, though it was an authority much challenged and somewhat precarious. When he was succeeded by two of his brothers, Edmund (939–46) and Edred (946–55), we come to the age of Dunstan in which the Archbishop of Canterbury becomes a national figure, as he had not been since the days of St Theodore three hundred years before.

St Dunstan's influence begins under Edred, but it reached its culmination when the two sons of Edmund succeeded each other. (Edred, like Athelstan before him, left no son.) It was Edgar, the second of these two sons of Edmund, whose reign (959–75) can be seen as the crown of Alfred's work. How serious were the strains and stresses which might have broken up the unity of the country is continually coming to light. Thus, when Edwy, the elder of Edmund's two sons, after only two years on the throne, was judged to be inadequate by the Northumbrians and Mercians, they joined forces against him and told him to make way, in their part of England at least, for his younger brother, Edgar. Edwy retained Wessex and ruled south of the Thames, while Edgar ruled the Midlands and the north. While generally it was a great misfortune that these kings died so young, it proved no misfortune that Edwy died almost immediately afterwards and the whole kingdom was united under Edgar. But it was still quite uncertain where the northern frontier of the domains of the King of the English, *Rex Anglorum*, was to be.

Edgar was crowned by St Dunstan at Bath, instead of at Kingston, in 973, only two years before his death and after he had been king for fourteen years. It looks as though the point of the ceremony was to proclaim that he was King of all England. When, after his coronation, he went north, he went by sea, sailing, presumably, from the Severn Estuary to the Mersey, and going from there to Chester to meet eight sub-kings, whom he had called on to attend him there. Of these eight the first was Kynath, King of the Scots, then Malcolm, King of the Cumbrians, Macchus, King of Many Isles (presumably the western islands of Scotland) and five others, whose names are given as Dufnald, Siferth, Huval, Jacob and Nichal, some of whom presumably ruled in Wales. These sub-kings rowed him on the River Dee, and Edgar, who steered the boat, was attended by a great concourse of his nobles. The whole occasion was an assertion of Saxon supremacy over the Celtic fringe of England, western Scotland and Wales.

Edgar was very conscious of the importance of sea-power, and the northern chronicler Simeon of Durham tells us that when he died, he had collected no fewer than 3,600 stout ships, divided equally into three parts to guard respectively the east, the west and the north of the island. But it is not clear whether the fleet allocated to the north was on the west to guard against the Danes in Ireland, or on the east to guard against incursions from Scandinavia.

Under Edgar, the union of England under one dynasty was so firmly established that it weathered the disasters of Edgar's hapless son, Ethelred the Unready, and the further outbreaks of violence between Saxons and Danes which might easily have resulted in a reversion to a kingdom divided. Instead of that, when a Danish king, Canute, succeeded Ethelred (after the brief reign of his own father, Sweyn, which lasted less than a year), it was generally accepted that Canute should not base his power on York but in the south. (The famous episode in which he reproved his courtiers' flattery by showing them the limitations of kingly power in the face of the inexorably in-coming tide took place on the south coast by Chichester, near where Alfred had so often resided.) It may well be true that the unity of the kingdom was in jeopardy again after the death of Edward the Confessor, when Harold's brother Tostig brought in the King of Norway with a view to making a separate kingdom in the north and leaving his brother Harold, already Earl of Wessex, to be king only of the old original Wessex. But Harold acted as though the threat in the north and the threat in the south were equal threats against the same kingdom, and William the Conqueror was no sooner established in the south than he went north and, by the brutal process known as the harrying of the north, brought the whole country under the government of Westminster, as it has since remained. Newcastle-upon-Tyne was the creation of William Rufus to the same end.

In this real sense, Alfred is to be regarded as the man chiefly responsible for the English Crown, which through all subsequent challenges and vicissitudes has meant that England, as distinct from Scotland and Wales, was governed throughout the Middle Ages from the south. This was largely due to the importance of the port of London, with its nearness to the Low Countries and the riches of northern France. Such words as 'staple', and measures like 'troy weight' and 'sterling' from the Easterlings or Hansa merchants reflect the steady economic preponderance which London was to acquire, so that whoever held London won the struggles between rival factions in the fifteenth no less than in the seventeenth century.

The century before Alfred, Offa, King of Mercia, had controlled London, and, as we have seen, exported English clothing to the Court of Charlemagne; the letters exchanged between the two rulers still exist. But then the Danes, coming up the Thames estuary and wintering for the first time in England in the isles of Thanet and (when Alfred was a small boy) Sheppey, must have greatly interfered with the trade of the port until Alfred's final and permanent inclusion of London as part of the kingdom over which he ruled. Even so, the Danes were never very far away, and the last wars of Alfred's reign were largely concerned with the defence of London. It was perhaps a relic of the long supremacy of Mercia over London (facilitated by Watling Street and the other Roman roads) that Alfred left its control in the hands of a Mercian *ealdorman*, his son-in-law. The *Anglo-Saxon Chronicle* tells us briefly that when this *ealdorman* died in 912, Alfred's son Edward took over London and Oxford. However, the silver pennies, five to the shilling (just as they have come to be today, except that today they are not silver), were minted at various centres, which indicates that there was not as yet any one city that deserved to be called the capital.

When Alfred translated Bede's *History*, he must have made a wry face when Bede at the end looks forward to the future, full of optimism at the growth of civilising influences:

> The Picts have now made a treaty of peace with the English nation, and rejoice in being united in Catholic peace and truth with the Church Universal. The Scots that dwell in Britain, content with their own bounds, neither plot nor conspire more against the English. The Britons, though they for the most part hate all

OPPOSITE David the harpist and attendant musicians from the eighth-century Canterbury Psalter.

OVERLEAF Two biblical stories from Caedmon's Genesis, *c.* 1000: RIGHT Noah's Ark: Noah is ready to steer; two of his sons and their wives are aboard, the third urges on his mother. LEFT Cain murders his brother Abel and replies to God's questioning 'Am I my brother's keeper?'

193

lazcaz rcxil· pxm onpximum pide leczan· hponne
me gemicce man rcylozne· reme frhon odde nhxh·
faehde gxmomge· bnxodon cpxilmfx· ic hir blxod aghxx·
onxon onxbnxdan· þu coxdæge þxrrum· adxmfx me
fnam ougxide· qadxpufxhx fnom· þxhide minum· me
co aldon banan· pxbxodxh pnadnxa pum· ic apxynxged
rcxil· þxbxodxh ofgexyhxde· þinne hpxonfan·

Noe ꝼꝛæme. ꝛþa hine neꝛᵹſꝛð heht. hynde þam hal
ᵹan. heoꝼon cyninᵹe onᵹan. oꝛoꝛt lice þ hoꝝ þyncan
micle mſꝑe ſyſte. maᵹum ꝛæᵹde. þ þæꝛ hꝛuſlic þinᵹ
þbodum toꝝſumd. ſeðe ꝑiꝛe. hie neꝛohton þæꝛ ᵹe
ꝛꝛꝛh þa ymb þincꝛa ꝑoꝛn. þæn ꝼæꝛt mætod. ᵹbꝼoꝛn
huꝛa mæꝛt. ᵹꝛno hliꝛiᵹſtan. maᵹꝛ iꝛuꝛan. tonðan
linie. ᵹeꝼæꝛmod ꝑið ꝼlode. þæꝛnoᵹ. þy ꝛeꝼſꝛan.
þiꝛ ꝛynduᵹ cynn. Symle bꝛð þy hꝛmoꝛꝛa þehꝛc hꝛꝛoh
þꝛꝛꝛꝛ. ꝛyꝼunꝛe ꝛæ ꝛꝛiꝛumaꝛ. ꝛꝛiðoꝛ bꝛuꝛud.

King Canute (Cnut) and
Queen Elgifu present a
cross to the New Minster
at Winchester. At the foot
are the monks of the
Minster and at the top
Christ with St Mary and
St Peter, the patrons of
the abbey.

196

English folk, and wrongfully, from wicked use, oppose the appointed Easter of the Catholic Church, yet can in no way prevail as they would, the power of God and of man alike letting them. For though in part they are their own masters, yet in part also are they under English sway. Such being the peaceful and calm state of the times, many lay aside their weapons, and incline ... to monastic vows rather than ... soldiership. What will be the end hereof the next age will show.

Bede never envisaged that the Tweed would become a frontier river dividing England from Scotland for centuries down to the present time. He knew that a Northumbrian king, Edwin, had founded Edwin's Burgh round its great castle, and presumably had not intended to make Edinburgh an outpost, but to extend his sway further north. Canute, who was the first king to call himself 'King of England' instead of 'of the English', would have had strong reasons for making York his capital. It would have been much more convenient for a ruler who was also ruling across the North Sea in Denmark, Norway and Sweden. That he did not do so but ruled from the south was because the throne he inherited was the throne of Wessex, as built by Alfred, his son and grandsons.

So great was the influence of St Dunstan in the monastic revival that the chroniclers, being themselves monks, were for a long time more interested in Edgar than in his great-grandfather, Alfred, who, as we have seen, had not much to boast of in the way of monastic foundations. He gave generously to monasteries in Ireland and on the Continent, but that was lost on the chroniclers of English abbeys. Edgar had made many endowments and although we may well believe that the inspiration came from Dunstan and his lieutenants, like Ethelwold of Winchester or Oswald of Worcester, the chroniclers are careful to give the credit to the King, so that the bishops, in replacing canons by monks, were carrying out the King's orders.

Probably because of the troubled state of the Papacy in the tenth century, no move seems to have been made for Alfred's canonisation. Henry II was descended twice over from Alfred: his grandfather, Henry I, was the son of the Conqueror's wife, Matilda of Flanders, who was descended from the fairest of

Parts of an Anglo-Saxon
reliquary *c.* 1050: Christ in
Majesty (left) and the
Virgin and Child.

OPPOSITE A Saxon
liturgical comb of the
ninth or tenth century.
It is made of ivory, carved
on the side showing with
Sagittarius and a ram. On
the reverse is a geometrical
and scroll ornamentation
inlaid with gold and
coloured glass.

Alfred's daughters who had married the Count of Flanders, the son of Alfred's stepmother, Judith. Henry II's grandmother, Henry I's first wife, was the daughter of St Margaret of Scotland, herself of Alfred's line. So when Pope Alexander III wanted to show his gratitude to Henry II for supporting him against the Emperor's anti-pope, he could have much better canonised Henry II's progenitor, Alfred, than Edward the Confessor, who was not a relation at all, save of the most distant cousinly kind. But the Confessor had an established reputation for sanctity, and he had paved the way for the Norman dynasty, and he was chosen. It is only too probable that Alexander III, though he did much to streamline and centralise the canonisation process, was ignorant of these relationships. So it was not until Henry VI, himself to be a candidate for this highest of honours, that an English king petitioned for Alfred's canonisation, and Henry VII did not pursue the matter. He was more interested in securing the canonisation of Henry VI himself, as his own uncle. For Henry VII, Winchester was the city not of Alfred but of King Arthur. He took care that his son and heir should be born at Winchester and christened Arthur, largely to please the Welsh to whom he owed so much.

But Alfred's fame never died. Already in the thirteenth century, the proverbs of Alfred began to circulate; wise and pithy sayings were attributed to him, under the heading 'Thus quoth Alfred'. There is extant a poem of this period embodying the proverbs, which may also include much older traditions for the vivid character it gives of the King, and the advice he gives in the poem to his son and heir. Alfred is called not only 'England's darling', but 'England's shepherd, England's King'. His advice to his son runs:

> My son, now I bid thee
> My dear one, my own
> Thou father thy folk,
> And be thou true Lord,
> To orphans be parent,
> To widows be friend,
> To poor men be comfort,
> To weak men be stay;
> And wronged men right,
> With all thy might.

200

The three kings following
Alfred, Edward, Athelstan
and Edgar, were worthy
successors who built the
English kingdom upon
Alfred's foundations. But
with the reign of
Ethelred II 'the Unready'
(right), the power of the
dynasty crumbled, and in
1017 the West Saxons
accepted the Danish
Canute as their king
(below right).

Canute ruled England and Denmark until 1035 but the kingdoms fell apart with the death of his son Harthacnut in 1042. A strong movement in England led by Earl Godwin brought Ethelred's son Edward back from exile to the throne. Edward the Confessor (above left) ruled from 1042–66 when he was briefly succeeded by Godwin's son, Harold II (left), before the Norman Conquest.

He was thought of as a law-giver, and in that capacity eclipsed his predecessors whose laws he had collected and codified, although he never received the eminence as a law-giver which it had suited William the Conqueror to attribute to Edward the Confessor. The Normans, frenchified and Romanised, and guided by the two great Italian prelates Lanfranc and Anselm, were setting their stamp on English law which to this day retains a number of old French phrases, including the royal assent to legislation. For that very reason it was important to emphasise the traditional and customary character of the Common Law, and over and over again the Normans had recourse to the formula 'in the time of King Edward' to under-line the notion of legal succession rather than the brutal realities of the Norman Conquest.

The last thing William the Conqueror would have wished was that his conquest of England should have become the most decisive date in English history. He had hoped to succeed as a relation of the Confessor, whose mother had been the daughter of a Duke of Normandy, William's great-grandfather – a tenuous claim in terms of consanguinity, but good enough when the monarchy was still largely a matter of popular con-sent (and three Danish kings with no Saxon blood had been accepted in the half-century before William secured the crown). Yet 1066 was curiously decisive, as is shown by the way in which Edward I was never called, as he should have been, Edward IV. He had three very notable Saxon predecessors: Edward the Elder who carried on Alfred's work through a quarter of a century of successful rule; Edward II, who was perhaps fortunate in being venerated as a martyr, though never formally canonised, and Edward III, the Confessor, the only English King to have been raised to the altars of the Church, and the King whose choice of Westminster, and shrine in the Abbey, was the decisive reason why the government of England came firmly to anchor at Westminster.

When, in the fullness of time, it became necessary for publishers to find a pictorial representation of Alfred, they ignored the contemporary evidence of the Saxon coinage which, rough and ready as its workmanship is, can presumably be trusted when it shows him as clean-shaven. Because he was thought of as a law-giver, the first imaginary portraits, late in the seventeenth century, show Alfred with a thin white beard, and this was repeated by the French artist Georges Vertue, when he did the illustrations for the *History of England* by Rapin de Thoyras, the Huguenot refugee who wrote in the early eighteenth century a history of England which marks a stage away from the chroniclers and towards the more scientific history of the nineteenth century. Hume and Smollett followed Rapin de Thoyras in telling the story of the political development of the kingdom, and by their day Alfred was secure in his distinction.

But it was in the nineteenth century that there really began the especial cult of Alfred, closely connected with the growing admiration for all things Germanic, by contrast with Latin Europe. The English had settled down under a German dynasty, continually refreshed with new blood from the Protestant princely and ducal families of north Germany. Queen Victoria's grandfather, George III, might have gloried in the name of Briton, but he also ruled in Hanover, and when the succession was in jeopardy and his sons had hastily to find wives, Queen Victoria's father found a German princess, and Queen Victoria herself a German husband, while her eldest daughter married the heir to the throne of Prussia. The Hanoverian tradition was military and autocratic, and soon showed itself in the character it gave to the British Army, but there also began a new development of the idea that law and constitution and the roots of British freedom were to be found in old Germanic customs. Alfred the Great fitted very well into this picture. A German scholar, Dr Pauli, a refugee from Germany after 1848, settled at Oxford, and devoted himself to Alfred the Great with more thoroughness than any English scholar had shown.

The millenary of Alfred's birth was celebrated in 1849 with an enthusiasm which was really extraordinary after a thousand years. An enormous crowd, variously estimated at anything from twenty to a hundred thousand people, gathered in the little town of Wantage, and from celebrations spread over three days, something highly practical resulted. A committee was appointed to bring out the Jubilee edition of all King Alfred's works, together with explanatory and elucidatory essays on his life, his laws and his coinage. The work took nine years to complete, but two fine volumes appeared in 1858,

with a popular poetaster of the time, Martin Tupper, rendering Alfred's Anglo-Saxon poems into Victorian rhyme. A statue was erected in Wantage, the work of Count Gleichen, a relation of Queen Victoria. As there were no contemporary portraits except the rough coinage, Count Gleichen copied the features of a local landowner and soldier, Lord Wantage, who had won the Victoria Cross in the Crimea, and this was probably more sensible than the engraving with a long white beard suggestive of the law-giver. A smaller statue was erected early in this century at Pewsey in Wiltshire, claiming Alfred as a great landowner in those parts. But his chief statue at Winchester was the result of massive celebrations of a thousand years after his death.

In the half-century since the celebrations of his birth, Alfred had been admirably served by a new school of Oxford historians who provided the historical knowledge of late Victorian England. John Richard Green, with his very popular *History of the English People*; both a long and a short version, celebrated Alfred, and taught that the Englishman's love of freedom came out of his Germanic roots. The future Bishop Stubbs provided detailed scholarship for all this early history, particularly as it affected the Church and the law. Above all, E. A. Freeman, Professor at Oxford till 1890, acclaimed Alfred as the most perfect ruler in history. The moving spirit in the celebrations was the Mayor of Winchester, Alfred Bowker, but he operated on a national scale, easily obtained Queen Victoria's approval and made the Lord Mayor of London hold more than one banquet. He looked across the Atlantic and received a warm message from President McKinley, ignoring the President's Celtic origin. Americans were encouraged to see their Constitution, no less than the British Constitution, as having its roots in Anglo-Saxon England, in which Alfred was the chief figure. The imposing statue of Alfred in Winchester was the practical result, carved by the most popular sculptor of the day, Thorneycroft, who had also made the statues of Boadicea and Richard Cœur-de-Lion at Westminster. The unveiling address was entrusted to a Scotsman, Lord Rosebery, but there were also organised series of scholarly lectures and addresses subsequently published, which have stood the test of time very well. As Queen Victoria died in January 1901, there were numerous

OPPOSITE King Alfred's statue at Wantage.

The traditional pride in
Alfred's achievements
expressed in a painting at
the Houses of Parliament
by Colin Gill: King
Alfred's longships defeat
the Danes.

comparisons between Alfred the Great and Victoria the Good, his reign of thirty anxious years with small resources and her splendid reign of sixty years, leaving the British Empire at the height of its power and extent, looked on as the mighty oak grown from the Anglo-Saxon acorn of a thousand years before.

It is not surprising that these Victorian Protestants tended to pass lightly over the details of Alfred's religion, his devotion to the Apostolic See of Rome, to the Mass and the Divine Office of the Church, and his veneration for relics, and they did not ask Alfred's co-religionists who were their contemporaries to take any part in these extensive commemorations. But it was Mr Bowker's essential achievement to make Winchester conscious of the great King. Ten years later a different and wider tribute was paid, such as poets alone can pay, when G.K. Chesterton recalled Alfred as the hero of his *Ballad of the White Horse* in 1911, a poem which celebrates the Christian virtue of hope, and uses the heathen Danes as figures of analogy for all the later heathen nihilistic enemies of the great Christian tradition built up by the holders of the Christian faith. On his title-page he transcribed from Alfred's translation of Boethius Alfred's own confession of faith: 'I hold, as do all Christian men, that it is a Divine Providence that rules, and not fate.'

But we may leave the last word with Florence of Worcester, writing about 1200:

> Alfred the king of the Anglo-Saxons, the son of the most pious king Ethelwulf, the famous, the warlike, the victorious; the careful provider for the widow, the helpless, the orphan and the poor, the most skilled of Saxon poets, most dear to his own nation, courteous to all, most liberal, endowed with prudence, fortitude, justice and temperance; most patient in the infirmity from which he continually suffered; the most discerning investigator in executing justice, most watchful and devout in the service of God.

A longer historical perspective, and all the scientific historical work of the last hundred years, have done nothing to diminish the justice of that high acclaim.

RIGHT The statue of Alfred at Winchester.

Chronology

of the main events in England from the end of the Roman occupation to the Norman Conquest

c. 410   Withdrawal of the Roman legions to the defence of Rome (sacked by the Goths 410) leaves the country divided into small kingdoms and open to attacks from Scotland, Ireland and the Continent.

425–58   Vortigern reigns in the largest of the British kingdoms. He uses Saxon mercenaries led by Hengist and Horsa to defeat the Picts but *c.* 441 the Saxons revolt against him and found their own kingdom, possibly Kent. Subsequently numerous fleets of settlers come from Germany: Angles, Saxons and Jutes.

c. 459   After heavy fighting the political leaders of the British are assassinated. Many of the surviving nobility emigrate to Gaul.

450–500   The British make a come-back under the leadership of Ambrosius Aurelianus the younger and Arthur.

495   Cerdic, a Saxon leader, takes Hampshire and the Isle of Wight from the Britons. (Alfred was of the House of Cerdic.)

500   Arthur wins a victory over the Saxons at the battle of Mount Badon.

515   Death of Arthur. Central government disintegrates and the regions fall into the power of warlords.

560   Ceawlin (great-grandson of Cerdic) organises a confederation to drive the Britons out of Wessex. By 600 the Anglo-Saxons have permanently mastered most of England which is divided into kingdoms with fluctuating power and boundaries. The Britons are driven into Wales and Cornwall.

597–604   St Augustine's mission begins the conversion of the English. Ethelbert of Kent, 'Bretwalda' or paramount ruler of England, is baptised. St Augustine is made Archbishop of Canterbury.

616   Death of Ethelbert; collapse of Kentish supremacy.

617–32   Beginning of Northumbrian supremacy under Edwin, who is baptised in 625.

632   An alliance between the pagan Penda of Mercia and Cadwallon of North Wales defeats the Northumbrian army. Edwin is killed.

633–41	Reign of Oswald restores Northumbrian power and Christianity. Oswald is made a saint after his death in battle against Penda of Mercia.
654	Oswiu, brother of Oswald, destroys Penda's last alliance in the battle of Winwaed.
664	Oswiu holds the Synod of Whitby to resolve the dispute over the dating of Easter. The Roman tradition is accepted in preference to the Celtic.
670	Death of Oswiu ends Northumbrian supremacy.
672	Birth of the Venerable Bede who spent his life in monasteries at Jarrow and Wearmouth. His *Ecclesiastical History of the English Nation* is the chief source of knowledge of the preceding centuries.
688–726	Ine, a descendant of Cerdic, establishes his line as kings of 'the West Saxons' in control of Dorset, Wiltshire and Hampshire. Ine draws up the earliest substantial code of laws to survive.
716–57	Ethelbald establishes the supremacy of Mercia.
735	Death of the Venerable Bede marks the end of the golden age of Northumbrian art and learning.
757–96	Reign of Offa of Mercia, who rules all England south of the Humber and whose son-in-law rules Northumbria. He trades with Charlemagne (crowned Holy Roman Emperor in 800), introduces the silver penny, codifies the laws and builds a dyke to mark the border with Wales.
c. 800	Scandinavian raids begin.
825	Egbert of Wessex (grandfather of Alfred) defeats Ceolwulf of Mercia at the battle of Ellendun. Wessex becomes the most powerful kingdom with suzerainty over Kent, Sussex and Essex.
836	Egbert is defeated by an army of thirty-five shiploads of Danes.
838	Egbert defeats the Danes and their Cornish allies at Hingston Down.
839	Ethelwulf succeeds Egbert as King of Wessex.
c. 849	Birth of Alfred, fifth son of Ethelwulf, at Wantage.
853	Alfred visits Rome and is honoured by the Pope.
c. 855–7	Alfred visits Rome with his father, who marries Judith, daughter of Charles the Bald, on the return journey.
860	Ethelwulf is succeeded by his eldest surviving son Ethelbald, who marries his stepmother Judith.

862–6   Ethelbert succeeds his brother Ethelbald.

866   Ethelred succeeds his brother Ethelbert.

867   A great Danish army takes York and ravages Northumbria and Mercia. Alfred marries Elswitha of Mercia.

871   The Danish army, moving south, is defeated by the Saxons at Ashdown but has later successes. Ethelred dies and is succeeded by Alfred, whose campaign is inconclusive. The Danes move north again.

878   A surprise Danish attack on the royal *vill* at Chippenham routs the Saxons. Alfred retreats to Athelney, reorganises levies and defeats the Danes at Ethandune. The Danish leader Guthrum is baptised and makes peace with Alfred at Wedmore.

880   The Danish army settles on the land in East Anglia.

886   Alfred occupies London and makes a treaty with Guthrum dividing England along the line of Watling Street from London to Chester.

887–93   Alfred learns Latin.

892–6   A large Danish force under Haesten invades England but fails to win any significant battle and eventually disperses.

892–9   Under Alfred's direction five major books are translated into Anglo-Saxon.

899–925   Alfred is succeeded by his son Edward the Elder who, with the help of his sister Ethelflaed, Lady of the Mercians, regains the midlands and the south-east from the Danes.

925–40   The reign of Edward's son Athelstan, who wins recognition of his kingship over northern England and harries Scotland.

940–6   Reign of Athelstan's brother, Edmund.

946–55   Reign of Athelstan's brother Edred.

955–9   Reign of Edmund's son Edwy. His brother Edgar rebelled against him and was proclaimed King of Mercia in 957.

959   The country is reunited under Edgar the Peacable on the death of Edwy. St Dunstan, Archbishop of Canterbury, leads the movement for monastic reform.

973   Edgar's supremacy is asserted by solemn coronation by Dunstan at Bath, after which he travels to Chester to meet eight sub-kings who row him on the river Dee.

975	Edgar is succeeded by his thirteen-year-old son Edward.
978	Edward is killed by supporters of his younger brother Ethelred, and venerated as a martyr. Ethelred 'the Unready' becomes king.
980	From this date renewed Danish attacks were successful in the face of Ethelred's inability to unite the English.
991	Heroic but unsuccessful Saxon defence of the coast at the battle of Maldon.
1013	The Danish king Sweyn lands at Sandwich and establishes his rule all over England. Ethelred flees to Normandy.
1014	Death of Sweyn and restoration of Ethelred.
1016	On death of Ethelred his son Edmund Ironside and Canute, son of Sweyn, fight for the kingdom. Edmund dies.
1016–35	Canute reigns over England and Denmark; for part of the time over Norway and Sweden too.
1035–40	Reign of Canute's son by Aelfgifu, Harold I.
1040–2	Reign of Canute's son by Emma, Harthacnut.
1042–66	Reign of Edward 'the Confessor', son of Ethelred the Unready.
1051	During a quarrel with his father-in-law, Earl Godwin, Edward designates William of Normandy as his successor. But after Godwin's death in 1052 his son Harold becomes leader of the army and in favour with Edward.
1066	On the death of Edward in January the English nobility makes Harold king. On 25 September Harold defeats a Norwegian invasion at Stamford Bridge. He marches south to meet William of Normandy at the battle of Hastings and is defeated and killed.

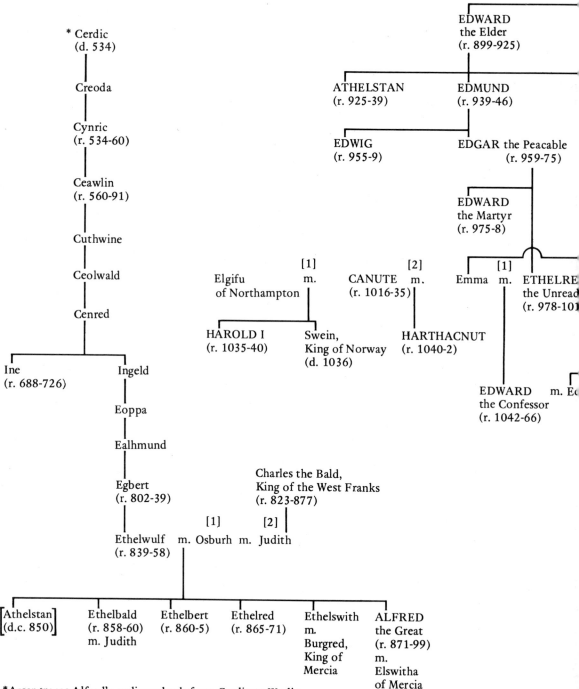

The Wessex Dynasty
from Cerdic to Alfred

The descent from Alfred the Great
to Henry II

* Cerdic
(d. 534)

Creoda

Cynric
(r. 534-60)

Ceawlin
(r. 560-91)

Cuthwine

Ceolwald

Cenred

Ine   Ingeld
(r. 688-726)

Eoppa

Ealhmund

Charles the Bald,
King of the West Franks
(r. 823-877)

Egbert
(r. 802-39)

[1]   [2]
Ethelwulf   m. Osburh m. Judith
(r. 839-58)

[Athelstan]   Ethelbald   Ethelbert   Ethelred   Ethelswith   ALFRED
[(d.c. 850)] (r. 858-60)   (r. 860-5)   (r. 865-71)   m.   the Great
              m. Judith   Burgred,   (r. 871-99)
                                                           King of   m.
                                                           Mercia   Elswitha
                                                                         of Mercia

EDWARD
the Elder
(r. 899-925)

ATHELSTAN   EDMUND
(r. 925-39)   (r. 939-46)

EDWIG   EDGAR the Peacable
(r. 955-9)   (r. 959-75)

EDWARD
the Martyr
(r. 975-8)

[1]   [2]   [1]
Elgifu   m.   CANUTE   m.   Emma   m.   ETHELRE
of Northampton   (r. 1016-35)   the Unread
                                                  (r. 978-101

HAROLD I   Swein,   HARTHACNUT
(r. 1035-40)   King of Norway   (r. 1040-2)
                (d. 1036)

                                      EDWARD   m. Ec
                                      the Confessor
                                      (r. 1042-66)

*Asser traces Alfred's pedigree back from Cerdic to Wodin
and the old Germanic gods.

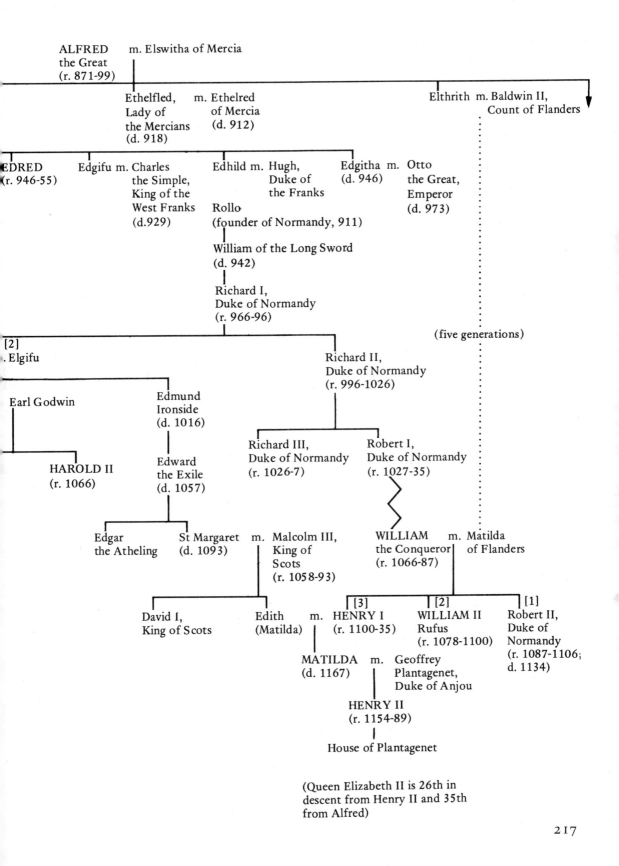

ALFRED
the Great
(r. 871-99)　　m. Elswitha of Mercia

Ethelfled,　　m. Ethelred
Lady of　　　　of Mercia
the Mercians　　(d. 912)
(d. 918)

Elthrith m. Baldwin II,
Count of Flanders

EDRED
(r. 946-55)

Edgifu m. Charles
the Simple,
King of the
West Franks
(d.929)

Edhild m. Hugh,
Duke of
the Franks

Edgitha m. Otto
(d. 946)　　the Great,
Emperor
(d. 973)

Rollo
(founder of Normandy, 911)

William of the Long Sword
(d. 942)

Richard I,
Duke of Normandy
(r. 966-96)

[2]
. Elgifu

Richard II,
Duke of Normandy
(r. 996-1026)

(five generations)

Earl Godwin

Edmund
Ironside
(d. 1016)

HAROLD II
(r. 1066)

Edward
the Exile
(d. 1057)

Richard III,
Duke of Normandy
(r. 1026-7)

Robert I,
Duke of Normandy
(r. 1027-35)

Edgar
the Atheling

St Margaret　m. Malcolm III,
(d. 1093)　　　King of
Scots
(r. 1058-93)

WILLIAM　　m. Matilda
the Conqueror│of Flanders
(r. 1066-87)

David I,
King of Scots

Edith　　m.
(Matilda)

[3]
HENRY I
(r. 1100-35)

[2]
WILLIAM II
Rufus
(r. 1078-1100)

[1]
Robert II,
Duke of
Normandy
(r. 1087-1106;
d. 1134)

MATILDA　m.　Geoffrey
(d. 1167)　　　Plantagenet,
Duke of Anjou

HENRY II
(r. 1154-89)

House of Plantagenet

(Queen Elizabeth II is 26th in
descent from Henry II and 35th
from Alfred)

217

Select bibliography

Every writer on Alfred must be deeply indebted to the specialist scholars who over the last hundred years have shed so much light on his life and times. There was a particularly fruitful crop at the beginning of this century, at the millenary of his death. From this period dates the standard text of Asser, published in 1904 by the Clarendon Press by W. H. Stevenson, a work so thorough that while it is constantly edited and re-printed with additional notes by later scholars, it is not likely to be superseded. The latest edition is dated 1959, which contains an article on recent work by Professor Dorothy Whitelock of Cambridge, whose own study, *The Genuine Asser*, was published by the University of Reading in 1968. With these, mention should be made of an important article in *History*, June 1971, by Professor R. H. C. Davis of Birmingham, 'Alfred the Great: Propaganda and Truth'. Virtually the whole of the second volume of R. H. Hodgkin's *History of the Anglo-Saxons* (OUP 1935) is the best full-length treatment of the reign known to me, though there are good briefer accounts in chapters VIII, IX and X of the second volume of the *Oxford History of England* by F. M. Stenton, and among the older historians, T. H. Hodgkin's volume I of Methuen's *Political History of England* and Charles Oman's *England before the Norman Conquest*.

The first volume of *English Historical Documents, 500–1000*, edited by D. Whitelock, contains a good deal relating to Alfred.

Extremely valuable is *The Life and Times of Alfred the Great* by Charles Plummer of Oxford, the Ford Lectures for 1901. Another Oxford scholar of that period, F. C. Conybeare, produced a very useful collection called *Alfred in the Chronicles*. Plummer's edition of the *Anglo-Saxon Chronicle*, contrasting in parallel columns the two main manuscripts, has been followed in an excellent Everyman edition of the *Anglo-Saxon Chronicle*, edited by G. N. Garmonsway, 1953, a most welcome exception to the general truth that at the moment it is not easy to find cheap and serviceable English versions either of Asser or of Alfred's own writings.

The Early English Text Society produced Gregory's *Pastoral Care* with a modern English version at the foot of each page. The Jubilee edition of Alfred's works, mentioned in chapter V, is now rare, but

King Alfred's translation of Boethius was issued with more literal translations of Alfred's own poems by Chatto & Windus in 1912. Asser's *Life* runs to only some forty pages, an inconvenient length for publishers. In the last century, Messrs Bohn issued an invaluable series of complete translations of the medieval chroniclers, and they included Asser in a volume called 'Six Old English Chronicles'. They also published English versions of William of Malmesbury, Henry of Huntingdon and Florence of Worcester, while *The Church Historians of England* series contains Simeon of Durham, but this series, which first appeared in 1840, is now rare. Bohn also published Dr Pauli's *Life of Alfred* in the same volume as Alfred's translation of Orosius. *The Short Chronicle of Ethelwerd* has lately been re-issued in Nelson's medieval text, a series to which those interested in Alfred look hopefully for more. *The Proverbs of Alfred* were issued in an edition prepared by the noted scholar W.W. Skeat by the Clarendon Press in 1907. The standard texts of all these chronicles, in Latin, is in the Rolls Series issued from the Public Record Office, and may be found in reference libraries.

There have been many biographies of Alfred in the last hundred years, but more in the first half of the century than the second. Mention may be made of one by Thomas Hughes (the author of *Tom Brown's Schooldays*) in the *Heroes of the Nations* series. Mr Bowker, the indefatigable Mayor of Winchester, published *Alfred the Great: Chapters on his Life and Times*, seven of the lectures given for the millenary, and he also published a volume on the millenary proceedings themselves. The late Alfred Duggan, a historical novelist who took great pains with historical detail, wrote about Alfred in *The King in Athelney*, Faber & Faber, 1961.

The Rome of Alfred's day is described in the third volume of Gregorovius' *History of the City of Rome in the Middle Ages*, and Hook's *The Lives of the Archbishops of Canterbury* has, in volume III, a full account of Plegmund. Of more specialised interest is *Alfred the Great and his Abbeys* by J. Charles Wall.

In *The Undergrowth of History* by Robert Birley, published by the Historical Association, there is a full discussion of the sources for the story of Alfred and the cakes. His possible connections with Oxford are examined in *The Early History of Oxford* by James Parker (Oxford Historical Society, 1885).

All that can be known about St Grimbald is to be found in *The English Historical Review*, October 1940.

Index

222